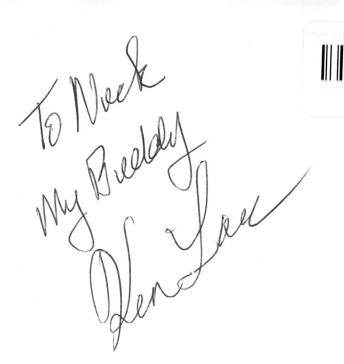

To Nicck
My Buddy

AuthorHouse™
1663 Liberty Drive, Suite 200
Bloomington, IN 47403
www.authorhouse.com
Phone: 1-800-839-8640

First published by AuthorHouse 12/5/2008

ISBN: 978-1-4389-3661-1 (sc)

Printed in the United States of America
Bloomington, Indiana

This book is printed on acid-free paper.

Forward:

The purpose of this book is to provide students, entrepreneurs, as well as, new and existing business owners and operators with significant information about the business side of business and more importantly by helping them:

1. Be more successful by assisting them in laying a solid foundation for: planning strategies; positioning, promoting, marketing, and advertising by way of traditional and internet media; economic development and cost savings.

2. How to address issues and relationships with employees and vendors; as well as other important information that will ultimately contribute to a more successful approach in the operation and economic growth of their business.

3. Protect their legal and financial interests with proper documentation.

About the Author

Ken Lane is a Graduate of the University of Pennsylvania with a degree in Architecture. He also Minored in theater arts, broadcast, and film communication, and has done post graduate study in Marketing Strategy at The University of Pennsylvania's Wharton School.

Ken has over twenty-five years of: experience in sales; marketing; business and product development; advertising; corporate communications; promotion; and public relations management.

Early in his career, Ken worked as an industrial, documentary, and commercial film writer, producer and director, of about 100 films, and has worked on several major motion pictures. He spent over eight years in radio and television as a writer, director, host, and producer of over 2,000 shows at: WIP-AM Radio in Philadelphia, WCMC-NBC-TV, AM & FM in Wildwood, NJ, and WLYF-FM Radio in Miami, FL.

He has held sales and marketing management positions with: Knight-Ridder News; Scripps-Howard Division of United Media Syndication; Industrial Training Systems Film & Video Productions; and Information Today Publishing. He was president and general manager of Burlington Marketing a marketing, advertising, public relations, & business consulting firm.

He served as Director of Online Services for Viacom's Simon & Schuster Higher Education Publishing Division where he was responsible for designing and building Prentice Hall's World Wide Web Site, for developing: a $60,000,000 Business Plan which included: a partnership with America Online, Distance Learning Programs with the New School University in NY, and digital information sales to University and Commercial Libraries.

He served as Director of Corporate Development for The Sports Network, an international sports news wire service that provides electronic worldwide delivery of sports news and other features about sports figures and events.

More recently he served as Operations and Data Acquisition Director for Corsearch, a trademark and intellectual property research firm.

Currently Ken heads up The Phoenix Group a Marketing & Business Consulting Company.

Ken has been a speaker and panelist at The National Online Meeting, The National Computer Machinery Association's Annual Conference, Mecklermedia's Internet World Conference, The New York Times Home and Office Conference and Expo, and Web Developers Conference.

He has appeared as an industry expert on national and international television programs and has been interviewed by a number of trade and professional journals, and was more recently interviewed for an article which appeared in *Open Computing Magazine*. He is the Author of "How to Avoid the Trials and Pitfalls of Building a Web Site in a Corporate Environment" and has just completed his latest book, "The Business of Doing Business."

Ken also, served as President of BNI (Business Networking Incorporated), a business networking consortium, and has Received Recognition Awards from: Sterling's Who's Who, The Special Library Association, The American Library Association, and is the recipient of The Broadcast Industry's Heart Fund and Cancer Society Citations.

Acknowledgments:

My thanks to:

Tom Erhardt, Esq. an attorney who specializes in business matters and heads up his own firm in Riverton, NJ, for reviewing and editing the legal issues discussed in this book.

Richard Marrella, staff writer with the Philadelphia Inquirer, **Laura Webb**, Editor of SJ Magazine, Marlton, NJ and **Elanor Farmer** of Farmer Press, Merchantville, NJ for their help with the proofing of this book.

Liz Lefkowitz, without who's tenacity and constant encouragement I would not have completed this body of work.

Malcomb Rosenberg, Esq. my colleague and personal Entertainment Industry attorney who heads up his own firm in Phila., PA, for his assistance in the final edit and suggestions about getting this project published.

THE BUSINESS OF DOING BUSINESS

A Handbook For Success In Business

by: Ken Lane

Contents

Outline for a Business Plan

Set goals for yourself and your company. It will force you to crystallize your thinking, taking into consideration everything that affects your business. You will have to analyze, assimilate, calculate, revise, and make decisions about the products and/or services your company provides, and how to make a profit through a marketing campaign. This is called a STRATEGY. There are three questions you should be able to answer.

1. What business are you really in?
2. What is happening in the business environment that could affect your business?
3. How do you organize all the resources you have (human, financial, material, etc.) to meet the business challenges ahead?
4. The plan should be typewritten including page numbers, an index for easy reference, a glossary if you are using words and terms that are foreign to potential investors, and a cover page outlining your intents.
5. The document should be inserted into a binding or cover.
6. Your plan should be approximately 25 to 50 pages long. The length depends on many factors, including type of business, supporting documentation, etc. Again, there is no set rule on the length of a business plan; 25 to 50 pages are simply used as an average.

Summary of the Proposed Venture

This should include the company's goals and purpose, the product features and market potential, capital requested, and technical and operational milestones.

Table of Contents
List the different sections of the plan. Organization of the plan will show something about your ability to organize a company. Management abilities are one of, and probably the most important, "keys" to funding by outside sources. "Anyone can come up with an idea, but we can take the idea and build a company around it."

Statement of Purpose
Outline the company overview, goals and objectives, company strategies, and critical success factors.

Operations Plan
Should include the background summaries of the principals, employee staffing requirements, a company organization chart, a product and service description, the purchasing and production planning overview, and critical success factors.

Marketing Plan
Should include a product and service description (in more detail than outlined in the Operations Plan), a market description, promotional strategy, pricing strategy, distribution channels, business location, analysis of competition and critical success factors.

Financial Plan
It will include the balance sheet, income statement, cash flow statement, sales statistics, staff additions, payroll expenses, capital additions, depreciation expense, debt amortization, accounts receivable, accounts payable, material flow, and detailed expenses.   All projections should be based on a five-year time period. The more comprehensive your plan is, the better your chances are of successfully obtaining the financing.

1. The Business Plan Objectives and Goals

A. Description of the business.
1. Type of business.

2. Status of business.
3. Business Form.
4. Why is your business going to be profitable?
5. Have you spoken with other people in this kind of business?
6. What were their responses?
7. What is special about your business?
8. How will you run the business?
9. When will (did) your business open?
10. What hours of the day and days of the week will you be in operation?
11. If business is seasonal, will the hours be adjusted seasonally?

2. The Marketing Plan

A. Basic Marketing Considerations.
    1. Who is your market?
    2. What is the present size of the market?
    3. What percent of the market will you have?
    4. What is the market's growth potential?
    5. As the market grows, does your share increase or decrease?
    6. How are you going to satisfy your market?
    7. How are you going to price your service, product or merchandise to make a fair profit and, at the same time, be competitive?

B. When you have a feel for your market, the following questions can be raised:
    1. How will you attract and keep this market?
      a. the image of the business
      b. pricing
      c. customer service policies
      d. advertising
    2. How can you expand your market?

C. Pricing considerations.
    1. What price do you anticipate getting for your product?
    2. In setting the price for your business, you must
    3. consider:

   a. cost of merchandise
   b. labor and operating costs
   c. planned profit
 4. Is the price competitive?
 5. Why will someone pay your price?
 6. How did you arrive at the price? Is it profitable?
 7. What special advantages do you offer that may justify a higher price (You do not necessarily have to engage in direct price competition.)?

3. The Location

A. Building, transportation, parking, and renovation considerations:

 1. What is your address?
 2. What are the physical features of your building?
 3. Is your building leased or owned? State the terms.
 4. If renovations are needed, what are they? What is the expected cost? Get quotes in WRITING from more than one contractor. Include quotes as supporting documents.
 5. What is the neighborhood like? Does the zoning permit your kind of business?
 6. What kind of businesses are in the area?
 7. Have you considered other areas? Why is this one the desirable site for your business?
 8. Why is this the right building and location for your business?
 9. How does this location affect your operating costs?
 10. Will the customer come to your place of business?
 11. How much space do you need?
 12. Will you want to expand later on?
 13. Do you need any special features required for lighting, heating, ventilation?
 14. Is parking available?
 15. Is public transportation available?
 16. Is the location conducive to drop-in customers?
 17. Will you pick up and deliver?
 18. Will travel time be excessive?
 19. Will you pro-rate travel time to service calls?

20. Would a location close to an expressway or main artery cut down on travel time?
21. If you choose a remote location, will you have to pay as much as you save in rent for advertising to make your service known?
22. If you choose a remote location, will savings in rent offset the inconvenience?
23. If you choose a remote location, will the customer be able to readily locate your business?
24. Will the supply of labor be adequate and the necessary skills available?
25. What are the zoning regulations of the area?
26. Will there be adequate fire and police protection?
27. Will crime insurance be needed and be available at a reasonable rate?

5. The Competition

A. What is the competition in the area in which you have chosen to locate your business?
1. The number of firms that handle your service?
2. Does the area appear to be saturated?
3. How many of these firms look prosperous?
4. Do they have any apparent advantages over you?
5. How many look as though they're barely getting by?
6. How many similar services went out of business in this area last year?
7. Can you find out why they failed?
8. How many new services opened up in the last year?
9. How much do your competitors charge for your service?
10. Which firm or firms in the area will be your biggest competition? List the reasons for your opinion.
B. Who are your five nearest competitors?
1. How will your operation be better than theirs?
2. How is their business? Steady? Increasing?
3. Decreasing? Why?
4. How are their operations similar and dissimilar to yours?

5. What are their strengths and/or weaknesses?
6. What have your learned from watching their operations?

6. The Management

A. This segment should include responses to the following questions:
1. What is your business background?
2. What management experience have you had?
3. What education have you had (including both formal and informal learning experiences) that has bearing on your managerial abilities?
4. Personal Data: age; where you live and have lived; special abilities and interests; reasons for going into business.
5. Are you physically up to the job? Stamina counts.
6. Why are you going to be successful at this venture?

B. Related Work Experience
1. Direct operational experience in this type of business.
2. Managerial experience in this type of business.
3. Managerial experience acquired elsewhere -- whether in totally different kinds of businesses, or as an offshoot of club or team membership, civic activities, church work, or some other source.

C. Duties and Responsibilities
1. Who will do what? Write major job descriptions.
2. What will be your form of legal organization?
3. What are your accounting needs? What records will you keep?
4. What are your insurance needs and what are the costs?
5. Who reports to whom?
6. Who makes the final decisions?
     a. Time for planning and reviewing plans.
     b. Major operating duties (purchasing, sales, personnel, promotion, production, and so forth as appropriate for your business)
     c. PLANNING.

D. Identify your major strengths and weaknesses.

6

E. Salaries (simple statement of what the management will be paid).
F. Resources available to the business
    1. Accountant
    2. Lawyer
    3. Insurance broker
    4. Banker
    5. List others, if applicable.

7. Personnel

A. What are your personnel needs now? In the near future? In five years?
B. What skills must they have?
C. Are the people you need available?
D. Full or part-time?
E. Salaries or hourly wages?
F. Fringe benefits?
G. Overtime?
H. Will you have to train people? If so, at what cost to the business (time of more experienced workers and money)

8. Application and Expected Effect of a Loan

A. How is the loan or investment to be spent?
B. What is (are) the item(s) to be bought?
C. Who is the supplier?
D. What is the price?
E. What is the specific model name and/or number of your purchase?
F. How much did you (will you) pay in sales tax, installation charges and/or freight charges?
G. How will the loan make your business more profitable?

9. Financial Data

A. Project a statement of income and expense.
B. Determine the financial requirements to get the business started.
    1. List all permanent assets required and the value or cost to obtain each.

a. inventory
b. equipment
c. leasehold improvements
d. automotive or trucks
e. fixtures
f. buildings
g. prepaid
h. etc.

2. Determine the working capital needs (cash), to get the business self-supporting.
   a. estimate one-time start-up expenses (non-asset).
   b. estimate monthly revenues and disbursements (cash flow) until the time that the business is self-supporting
   c. estimate contingency fund-safety factors.
   d. total cash needs will equal the highest cumulative negative cash balance in b., plus a. and c. above. Or: start-up expenses + largest cumulative cash operating
      deficit + contingency fund = cash needs

C. List the money and/or value of assets you intend to invest in the business (owner's equity).
D. Project your financing needs:
   Value of permanent assets + Working capital = Total funds needed - Your investment = Total financing required.

Marketing & Your Business Plan

Marketing plays a vital role in successful business ventures. How well you market your business, along with a few other considerations, will ultimately determine your degree of success or failure.

The key element of a successful marketing plan is to know your prospects—their likes, dislikes, and expectations. By identifying these factors, you can develop a marketing strategy that will allow you to arouse and fulfill their needs. Identify the demographics of your customers by their age, sex, income, educational level, and place of residence. Initially, target only those prospects who are more likely to purchase your product or service. However, as your customer base expands, you may need to consider modifying the marketing plan to include secondary markets as well.

Develop a marketing plan for your business by answering these questions. Your marketing plan is almost always included in your business plan and should contain answers to the questions outlined below:

1. Who are your customers? Define your primary and secondary target markets.

2. Are your markets growing, steady, or declining?

3. Is your market share growing, steady, or declining?

4. If you are a franchise, how is your market segmented?

5. Are your markets large enough to expand?

6. How will you attract, hold, and increase your market share?

7. How will the Internet attract, hold, increase your target markets?

The Business Plan

Competition is a way of life. We compete for jobs, promotions, scholarships to institutions of higher learning, in sports—and in almost every aspect of our lives. Nations compete for the consumer in the global marketplace as do individual business owners. Advances in technology can send the profit margins of a successful business into a tailspin causing them to plummet overnight or within a few hours. When you consider these and other factors, you can only conclude that business is a highly competitive, volatile arena. Because of this volatility and competitiveness, it is important to know your competitors. Answers to the following questions can help you be more competitive in today's marketplace:

1. Who are your five nearest direct competitors?

2. Who are your indirect competitors?

3. How are their businesses: steady? increasing? decreasing?

4. What have you learned from their operations? from their advertising?

5. What are their strengths and weaknesses?

6. How does their product or service differ from yours?

You should maintain a file on each of your competitors. Save copies of their advertising, promotional materials, and their pricing strategy. Update and review these files systematically, with the objective of determining when and how often they advertise, sponsor promotions or events and offer sales. Analyze the copy they use in their advertising, promotional materials, and sales strategy. For example: is their copy short, descriptive, catchy, and how much and how often do they reduce prices for sales? Using these procedures can help you to understand your competitors better and how they operate their businesses.

Marketing Planning for Small Businesses

A growing number of small business owners and professional advisers agree that marketing is the key factor determining success or failure in competitive markets. Venture capitalists often insist on having an experienced marketing executive on the management team prior to a commitment to full financing. In recent years, major high-technology organizations have replaced their technically educated founder/CEO's with professional managers who have a background and experience in large consumer marketing organizations.

Why this emphasis and interest in marketing? The answer lies in understanding the concept of marketing: the process which converts the firm's human, material, and financial resources into products or services that fulfill the market's needs as the consumer understands those needs. The degree of fulfillment and the cost-effectiveness of the process will determine a company's long-term profitability.

Marketing includes the sales, advertising, promotion, and publicity activities (the communications program) normally associated with marketing. Marketing is thinking and planning about what ought to be done in the future, which can be just the next three to twelve months in some high-growth markets. Sales are the major force in implementing a company's program. The communications program serves to make the selling effort more efficient and cost-effective.

One of the most critical characteristics of highly competitive markets is the rapid obsolescence of products and services. It is an absolute certainty that the nature of the market in the near future will be significantly different from that of today's market. If a company's sales and its communications program are not based on previous marketing "thinking," then the company will simply be reacting and allowing market-oriented competitors to "call the shots" and effectively control it.

Entrepreneurs have a natural and strong bias toward action. Lack of sales many times is not the result of poor sales techniques but the failure to offer a product or service that meets the market's requirements. Action without effective planning is a sure road to failure.

Sources of Information

Marketing planning need not be time-consuming and expensive. For the most part, marketing planning is a common sense way of understanding customers and potential customers and where the company best fits into the market-place. Small business owners and managers working with their sales organizations and customers should be able to perform most of their own marketing planning. Most of the information needed for a marketing plan is available free of charge from a variety of local sources such as: Libraries, Department of Commerce and Community Affairs, Small Business Administration (SBA), US Department of Commerce, Local Colleges & Universities, and Trade Associations. The use of outside professional experts can be helpful, but they should not be a substitute for management's marketing planning responsibilities.

To successfully convert company resources into products that fulfill market needs presumes an accurate understanding of the marketplace. Developing that understanding is a matter of asking and accurately answering a series of common-sense questions:

1. Who are my current and potential customers?
2. What determines their needs?
3. How have their needs changed in the recent past?
4. What is likely to be the nature of their needs in the next 12, 18, 24 months?
5. How much do they buy?
6. How often do they buy?
7. What is the acceptable price range for my type of products or services?

From the preceding information, one should be able to answer the three key questions that every organization of any size must ask:

1. What products/services should I keep?

2. What new products/services should I add?

3. What products/services should I eliminate?

The next set of questions deals with the other half of the marketing concept — a company's capability to compete profitably.

1. Which of the needs of my customers and potential customers can my company fulfill—at or very close to—the lowest industry cost of sales?

2. Where do these customers look for product information?

3. For which of my customer's needs is my sales and distribution organization well suited and cost-effective?

4. Who are my direct competitors, and how do they operate?

5. What is the likely trend of improvement in the main technologies that underlie product and services development in my business operation?

With this information, one should then be able to answer the three key marketing questions every organization of any size must answer:

1. What market segments/niches can I potentially dominate?

2. What type of selling program will be most effective and within my organization's competence?

3. What type of communications program will be required to insure adequate awareness of my products or services so that I can maximize the effectiveness of my selling effort?

Common Set of Problems

In my experience, marketing programs that fail tend to have a common set of problems:

1. A lack of consistency. Effective marketing requires an ongoing commitment, not just at a time when extra funds are available.

2. Spreading of too few dollars over too ambitious a program. Whatever is done should be done well consistently.

3. Expectation of an immediate profit payback from the marketing investment. Marketing activities have a cumulative effect. While it is reasonable and necessary to expect significant immediate results, marketing plans should not be evaluated in the short run on a strict return-on-investment basis.

4. Inappropriate marketing plan goals. Profit goals are part of the firm's overall plan because profits are the result of the firm's total performance. Marketing plans should focus on such goals as total unit sales, number of customers purchasing, orders per customers, first-time orders, repeat orders, system sales, and market share or penetration if appropriate.

Service Business Marketing

The following is a model to help you plan and clarify your marketing direction. Each element below has a list of questions to consider when you develop your marketing strategy. Using this information should help you to develop your marketing strategy.

1. Communicate with your prospects exactly why they should do business with you.

2. Package and present your services to generate interest and response from qualified prospects.

3. Develop more qualified prospects who are ready to do business with you now.

4. Turn those who call you into immediate sales...often over the phone.

5. Keep clients coming back and referring others to you...forever.

Positioning Your Business

1. What exactly is your business solution? That is, how does your service solve a particular problem, alleviate a pain or add value?

2. Who exactly are your potential clients or customers? Where are they; what industry; what size; what needs; what past experience with your kind of service and what buying process?

3. What is your unique customer advantage? That is, what differentiates you from your competitors? What do you do better, different, faster, cheaper, with higher quality or with a different spin? Be specific, not vague.

4. What is your business identity? What are the qualities you want to be known by? Is it integrity and dependability or expertise and exclusiveness? You can't be everything to everybody. Next ask what you are going to do to live up to these qualities.

5. What is your "phrase that pays?" What words concisely sum up your positioning strategy in a way that is memorable and meaningful, with both style and content. For Action Plan Marketing it is: "We help you find new clients without spending a fortune."

Packaging Your Services

1. Do you have an attractive and appropriate business identity package consisting of a logo or company masthead on business cards, letterhead and envelopes? This look for your business needs to express your identity and positioning strategy.

   Do you have basic marketing materials (fact sheets or brochures) for your business? These materials should include (but not necessarily be limited to): An overview of the problem that you are a solution for; an overview of your solution; a description of your unique customer advantage; a listing of your key customer benefits; a listing of your various services; testimonials from satisfied clients; a listing of clients or client companies; biographies of company principals; information on how to contact your company and how to do business with you; your address, phone, fax and e-mail.

2. Have you developed a basic strategy for the services you'll offer and what the configuration of those services will be? A three-day workshop; monthly executive coaching and team building retreats. All of these are packages. They need to be clearly defined and laid out.

3. Do you have a basic logistical plan for your business? A plan for the office; office hours; telephone message; signage, etc. All of these simple things convey a marketing image to your prospective clients. Create an identity and then package this identity in everything you do.

4. Have you put some attention on your personal package, your personal presentation? If you're a small service business you are selling you. You're the package. People make a dozen or more assumptions about you and your business in the first few seconds after meeting you in person or talking to you on the phone. Are you walking your talk?

Promoting Your Services

1. Are you networking enough? For many service businesses, networking is the key promotional technique. Join organizations, get to know people; get involved; keep in touch with people; do what you can to help them; be visible in your community.

2. Do you have a good, solid marketing letter that highlights your benefits and moves people to take action? This one inexpensive marketing tool is one of the most powerful when written properly.

3. Do you do personal PR such as speaking and writing? Again, these do not take much money but pay big dividends. Speak at Rotary Clubs, your Chamber of Commerce, at business associations and alumni groups. Write for your local paper; the trade journal of your industry, or even for someone else's newsletter. You can use the reprints later for credibility.

4. Are you utilizing your mailing list? This is an absolute must. Do not let people forget who you are and how you can help them. From two to six times a year, send clients and prospects a brochure, newsletter, or other type of keep-in-touch mailing.

5. Do you have a Web Site? You should. It doesn't take a lot of money to create a Web page and even less to post it. This is a powerful marketing media tool that can serve as a combination direct mail piece, brochure, and newsletter. Given the price of entry, it's crazy not to have one.

The Persuasion Process

1. Do you have a verbal logo? When someone asks, "what do you do?" do you have a concise and powerful solution statement that expresses what you do in a nutshell? A good format is "I help (who your clients are) to (what your solution is).

2. Do you have a basic phone approach scripted out? Whether you get incoming calls or make outgoing calls, you need to have a track to run on that takes the call from interest to action. Script it out. Include questions, comments, stories, and closes.

   Are people interested in what your business can do for them? They'll be much more interested if you're interested in them first. Find out who your prospects are; their situation; their challenges; their problems; their goals. And then really listen. Really be interested. What naturally follows is their interest in what you can do for them.

3. Do you know how to generate desire for your services? Nothing generates desire better than success stories about successful projects. Have them at the ready for over-the-phone or in person meetings.

4. Do you wait for people to take action or do you move the action forward? You've got to ask; you've got to recommend; you've got to suggest. However, do not ever be pushy or obnoxious. On the other hand, it can be just as irritating when dealing with a salesperson who never asks for the sale.

Performance in Your Business

1. Have you found a way to fit marketing into your schedule? Marketing is not a luxury; it's a necessity. You must find ways to do a little marketing on an ongoing basis. This may be only a few calls a week and a mailing every few months. But you must do it!

2. Do you keep track of both your long and short-term projects (including marketing projects), and review that list daily? Do you prioritize your projects and work on those first that have the highest payoff?

3. Do you have a way of combating procrastination and delay? There is nothing worse than generating work through effective marketing and then getting behind in the work you have generated.

4. Do you maintain the highest standards of integrity and excellence? Do you under-promise and over-deliver or visa versa? Your clients will judge you, not on what you promise but, on what you actually do.

5. Are you continually working to improve your skills in all areas of your business? Keep up your reading and education for your core professional skills while expanding your knowledge in other areas. Marketing, selling, negotiation, computer, financial and communication skills are important to every business.

Placing A Value on A Business
That You Are Considering Buying

Just as beauty is in the eye of the beholder, the value of a business may be perceived differently by each person involved in its sale and acquisition. Furthermore, the "value" should be isolated from the purchase price and the terms of the acquisition since value can be viewed in varied ways. Typically, the purchase price, or the manner of its determination, will be negotiated. Both parties to the transaction will want to consider the various particulars of value in order to maximize their positions.

Often, parties to the transaction will use the concept "fair market value"— as if there were some intrinsic value to an enterprise. However, the concept of fair market value is merely both sides to a transaction. This concept assumes a willing buyer and a willing seller, with neither party being under any compulsion to buy or sell. It also assumes that both parties will have reasonable knowledge of all relevant facts relating to the business.

The importance of reasonable knowledge of the relevant facts cannot be overstated. Supposedly, the seller of the business will have great access to the information, although reliance on that assumption may be detrimental to the seller. This information can be generally grouped into two categories: external factors and internal factors. External factors may include the relevant market, competitors, general condition of the economy, location service area, suppliers, customers, and financing availability. Internal factors may include employees, facilities, equipment, systems and procedures, and general efficiency of the operations. All sources of this information should be used, not merely information provided by the seller. Talk with the people or companies that will impact on the future operations of the business. Little harm can be done by talking with the potential suppliers, customers, and, yes, even the competition. The financial statements for the business are another crucial element of information. However, the financial

21

information should be examined with a profuse skepticism to determine how realistic it is. Questions about the financial statements include whether they are audited, whether the principles on which the financial statements have been prepared have been applied consistently, whether they are cash or accrual, and just how realistic this financial information is.

Once all the information has been gathered, it needs to be evaluated in the context of determination of the value. Various concepts are used in viewing the "value" of the business. Among these are the liquidation or asset value and the going concern value of the business.

Liquidation value means what the remaining assets would be worth after all the debts of the business were paid. This may or may not correspond to the book value, which generally is an aggregate of the excess of the assets of the company over its liabilities determined from the balance sheet. "Tangible" book value is another technique that considers the tangible assets. This merely states one beginning point, however, of evaluation because it is necessary to examine how the various assets themselves are valued on the balance sheet.

Depreciation from cost as well as changes in market value can have a substantial effect. Inventory may be stated on a "LIFO" or "FIFO" basis. Simply stated, LIFO valuation is based upon a concept of last in, first out, and FIFO is based on the principal of first in, first out. Intangible assets, which may or may not be expressed on the balance sheet, must be considered. For example, the trademark or name of the business may have a substantial value to which no amount is attributed. The term "good will" may or may not have any worth. Accounts receivable should be viewed with respect to collectability and age. The liabilities on the balance sheet must also be considered carefully. For example, does the business have continuing contracts such as leases which are not a liability expressed on the balance sheet, but for which the business has an on-going obligation? Another example concerns contingent liabilities, such as potential product liability claims, which could be asserted in the future.

All of these factors, and many others, must be taken into consideration in using the balance sheet or assets to fix a "value."

Another means of valuing a business looks at the "going concern value." This takes into consideration the future earnings prospects. A business with few assets may have great potential for earnings and thus be highly valuable. On the other hand, a business with substantial assets may have little prospects for earnings growth. A price earnings ratio or multiple of earnings is a concept sometimes used. It may be stated that, if earnings are $100 for a year, the value of the business is $1,000, or ten times its earnings. Various businesses can have different multiples. In addition, various factors must be considered in evaluating the historical earnings of the business. For example, has the owner of the business taken a high or a low salary out of the business? How realistic are expenses? How much has been spent on maintenance? What is the likelihood of growth in earnings? Have the earnings been receding? What external factors can impact on the earnings? All of the items of the income statement need to be evaluated to determine whether the earnings shown and the future potential for earnings are realistic.

Cash flow of the business is another consideration in evaluation. Cash flow is the working capital generated from operations...the net income plus the non-cash expenses minus non-cash income. A business with a high cash flow or potential for high cash flow may have greater value.

There is no one way to value every business and no absolute "value" of any business. All of the factors must be taken into consideration, including the goals and objectives of the purchaser and the seller. Whether the purchase price is to be paid in cash or in installments makes a difference in value. Tax benefits available to the parties that can be achieved by a specific structure for the transaction should be considered as well as other factors. Often the seller desires to stay active on a lesser basis and wants to be assured of an employment or consulting agreement. This opportunity may not change the value of the business, but can affect the purchase price. Similarly, assets may be separated by selling them or having the seller retain them and lease them to the purchaser. All this is to say that even once the value is determined, the purchase price may be changed depending on the terms of the transaction. All of the factors must be considered in order to arrive at an agreement for the sale of the business. Good advice to the parties on these issues from legal counsel, accountants, and other advisers can be very important to achieving a desirable result.

About Incorporating

If you are planning to start your own business or are in business as a sole proprietor or partnership you might want to consider the pros and cons of incorporating your business. There are, of course, many factors to consider and I suggest that you consult with a professional before making any decision about incorporating and the type of corporation that is best suited for your particular type of business. The following are just a few highlights and considerations:

The Up Side:

1. Limited personal liability—By far, the overwhelming reason why businesses incorporate is to help protect their personal assets--home, car, family savings, etc.--from business debt. No one can attach your personal assets if your business fails or you lose a lawsuit. This "limited liability" feature of corporations is not available in a sole proprietorship or partnerships, where the individual or partners are personally liable for all debts of the business.

   Tax saving options for a corporation far out number those available to sole proprietorships and partnerships. For example, you can establish pension, profit sharing and stock ownership plans, thus lowering the corporation's taxable income. Medical, life and disability insurance premiums can be completely tax deductible for the corporation. Also, a corporation may own shares of stock in another corporation and receive 80% of the dividends...tax-free!

2. Ease of transferring ownership. For example, if an owner of a corporation dies, the ownership portion can be quickly transferred and the corporation can continue to operate.

3. Estate and family planning becomes easier because shares of a corporation can be easily distributed to family members.

4. Increased ability to attract outside investments. A corporation can also raise capital by issuing stocks, bonds or other securities.

5. There is greater ease in doing business for a corporation, in fact suppliers and banks favor corporate accounts and many may even offer corporate discounts.

6. Continuity of business: A corporation is the most enduring form of business structure.

The Down Side:

1. Increased paperwork and record keeping.

2. Net income of the business may be insufficient to take advantage of corporate tax benefits

3. Limited personal liability advantage may be circumvented by creditor requirements of a personal guaranty

TYPES OF ENTITIES TO CONSIDER:

General Business Corporation: Private Type
Although the most formal corporate structure, this type is the most widely used by both small and large businesses and offers the fewest restrictions. This structure is most suitable to the corporation which plans to have more than 30 shareholders and which plans to make large public stock offerings.

Close Corporation:
There are a few minor but significant differences between general corporations and close corporations. In most states where close corporations are recognized, they are limited to 30 stockholders. Also, when selling stock, it may have to be first

offered to existing shareholders. This type of corporation is particularly well suited to the entrepreneur who wants to be a one-person corporation, or a small group of individuals who will all participate in running the business.

S Corporation:

Many business owners find the S corporation especially attractive in that all earnings or losses are passed through directly to their personal income tax return. As a result, it avoids the double taxation feature of general business and close corporations. Certain requirements must be met before qualifying for S corporation status, and we recommend that you consult with your tax advisor before electing S corporation status. To obtain the special S corporation tax status, the corporation must have all shareholders sign IRS Form 2553 and this form must be filed with the IRS within 75 days of the date of incorporation.

Limited Liability Company: LLC

This type of business entity has recently emerged as a superior alternative to corporations and partnerships. The Limited Liability Company (LLC) combines the best features of corporations and partnerships: the corporate advantage of limited personal liability and the taxation advantage of partnerships. The LLC is now recognized in most states and is a highly flexible business entity created in response to the demand for a better alternative to traditional forms of business.

WHERE SHOULD I INCORPORATE?

It is amazing that Delaware, the 2nd smallest state in America, is the home of nearly 60% of the companies listed on the New York and American stock exchanges and over half of the Fortune 500 firms. Also, many international companies looking to do business in the US and in other jurisdictions worldwide choose Delaware because of its corporation law structure, its stability and its reputation as the "American Corporate State."

Delaware is also one of the least costly state in which to incorporate. The cost to incorporate in Delaware can vary from only $99, which includes most Registered Agents service fee and all state fees. With the corporate kit, the complete cost starts at about $179. Average Incorporation and LLC services can cost about $298, including the Registered Agent fee for the first year; and ongoing Registered Agent service costs start at about $75 per year. And, yes! You do need a Registered Agent to file in Delaware.

Your Delaware Corporation is what is known as a "domestic" corporation in Delaware. In other states, it is considered a "foreign" corporation. Depending on the nature of the business, you may have to register your Delaware Corporation in the state in which you plan to maintain offices, hire employees and transact business. Because of Delaware's many corporate advantages and low annual franchise tax, many businesses prefer to operate as a Delaware corporation in their home state.

Furthermore, your business does not need to maintain a bank account or any offices in Delaware as long as a professional registered agent represents you. Currently, nearly a quarter million companies are registered in Delaware and few have ever visited the state. However, Delaware may not be the best state for you to incorporate your business. For example: your own state may require you to "qualify" as a foreign company. This qualifying process involves procedures and costs similar to incorporating. So, you may want to consider incorporating in your home state to avoid the additional cost. In many cases, the costs that are involved in qualifying can outweigh the advantages gained from the state of incorporation.

For more information about incorporating in Delaware you may want to surf the Web for agent's sites. There are just too many to list here, so just go to one of your favorite search engines and type: "incorporating in Delaware" in the query box, and you should get at least a dozen or more sites that you may want to visit.

Advantages of a Nevada Corporation

1. No Corporate Income Tax
2. No Corporate Shares Tax
3. No Personal Income Tax
4. No IRS Information-Sharing Agreement
5. Nominal Annual Fees
6. Minimal Reporting And Disclosure Requirements
7. No Franchise Tax
8. Stockholders Are Not Public Record

Additional Advantages

1. Stockholders, directors and officers need not live or hold meetings in Nevada

2. Directors need not be stockholders.

3. Officers and directors of a Nevada corporation can be protected from personal liability for lawful acts of the corporation.

4. Nevada corporations may purchase, hold, sell or transfer shares of its own stock.

5. Nevada corporations may issue stock for capital, services, personal property or real estate, including leases and options. The directors may determine the value of any of these transactions, and their decision is final.

An incorporated business has many more advantages for its owners than a sole proprietorship or partnership. One of the primary reasons to consider incorporation is the limited liability aspect not found in some other forms of business enterprise. An owner in a corporation is known as a stockholder. A stockholder's personal liability is limited to the amount of capital invested in the corporation. Shares of stock are issued and represent the corporate owners' interest in the business.

While there have been cases where the Internal Revenue Service or creditors of a corporation have successfully pierced the corporate veil, the stockholder's personal liability is protected–if the corporation is properly organized and operated–from corporate lawsuits and subsequent financial losses. The fact that a great percentage of new businesses go bankrupt within a short time should be enough incentive for a new business owner to seriously consider the advantages of incorporation. When starting a new business, you would be foolish not to take into consideration the possibility of failure.

This risk factor should be taken into account far in advance and not as an afterthought that comes too late. New entrepreneurs really do not want to believe ventures will fail, but statistics tell us otherwise. The larger the venture the more reason to incorporate. Other advantages to incorporating your business follow.

1. Shares of stock may be used for estate and financial planning, including ownership by an offshore corporation or asset protection trust (APT).

2. Distribution of stock to family members or transfer of ownership to others can be transacted smoothly without interruption or dissolution of business. Stock certificates are personal property. To initiate a change of ownership, simply endorse the back of the certificate, unless restricted by articles of incorporation, bylaws or shareholder agreement.

3. Investors prefer investing in a corporation.

4. Corporate profits can be accumulated for business purposes as permitted by the Internal Revenue Service. This way profits do not have to be distributed immediately, and shareholders can postpone paying taxes on the money, if they choose to do so.

5. The corporation is a legal entity, the same as an individual, but created by statute. It can sue and be sued in the name of the corporation.

6. A corporate entity is much more organized. Management is elected by a majority. Corporate meetings and major decisions are conducted by a board of directors elected by the shareholders. Officers are then appointed or elected by the directors to carry out the daily operations of the business. Frequently, the stockholders, directors, and officers are the same person or persons. However, by doing business under the formal structure of a corporation, the business can organize expansion with proper leadership and responsibilities being administered by qualified parties in orderly succession.

7. You might elect to become an S corporation; in doing so, profits are taxed essentially the same as a partnership or proprietorship.

8. The Internal Revenue Code allows shareholders to deduct stock loss from personal income, up to a specified amount, under Section 1244. Even with failure, investors can still benefit.

9. The corporation can provide health, medical, and disability insurance plans for employees and write off the cost as a business expense. The benefits of these plans are not taxable to the employee/shareholder.

10. Tax deductible medical and dental reimbursement plans can be established for employee/stockholders.

11. Pension, profit-sharing, stock-option, and term life insurance plans can be made available to employee-stockholders.

12. Some institutions will not deal with an unincorporated business.

If those are not enough reasons to incorporate, here are a few more to think about. The following is a partial list of tax deductible corporate expenses:

- Advertising
- Legal fees
- Discounts to customers
- Automobile expenses
- Business licenses
- Entertainment
- Factoring costs
- Bad debts
- Pension plans
- Financial consultants
- Bonuses
- Patents
- Invoicing
- Contributions to profit sharing
- Limited partnership costs
- Logo & trademark design Costs
- Telephone
- Copyrights

- Depreciation
- Accounting costs
- Moving expenses
- Employees wages
- Machinery and equipment
- Books
- Office expenses
- Finders' fees
- Business consultants
- Printing costs
- Insurance
- Commissions
- Travel
- Incorporation costs
- Worthless securities
- Director's fees
- Workman's comp insurance
- Medical/dental reimbursement plans

Tax deductions change frequently so an accountant should be consulted for up-to-the-minute information.

For more information about incorporating in Nevada and the nominal fees involved, the following company can answer any questions you might have, and will also help to get you started in your incorporating process.

CRA of America, Inc.™
3638 Rancho Drive, Suite 6 - Las Vegas, Nevada 89130
Telephone (702) 243-9150 - Fax (702) 243-6896
www.craofamerica.com.

Developing A Mission Statement

It is incumbent upon anyone who is contemplating starting a business or who may have previously established a business that you consider developing a clearly defined mission for your enterprise. One that covers what your business is all about and how you go about conducting business.

Over time this mission might expand or contract depending upon your company's situation. However, you certainly will want to start from the perspective of a clearly defined mission, and while you're at it, you'll also want to address such issues as expectations vs. reality!

Additionally, you need to be acutely aware that with the diversity of opinion in most business settings—it might be a good idea to bring all the people involved in the success or failure of your venture together for a meeting of the minds to hammer out the vision of your company's mission. This group should include anyone and everyone who will be involved in the process...I might also suggest that you might want to follow these basic steps to operationalize your mission statement.

1. Craft a statement that answers some basic questions such as:

   A. What business activities will the company be involved with in, say, one - three and five years? Get a clear picture of what and where you want your company to be in the long term...and start planning and operating the business as if you were already there.

   B. What are our objectives?

   C. How will we reach our goals?

1. Communicate your company's mission throughout the entire organization and make absolutely sure that everyone in the company understands how this mission will effect everything they do and how they go about doing their jobs on a day-to-day basis.

2. Translate key elements of your mission into relevant performance objectives for employees at all levels of your operation.

3. Every important decision that you make about your business operation should be tested against your mission with questions such as: how will this decision effect our objectives, will it help meet our goals, etc. If the decision you are about to make will adversely effect your goals and objectives, you had better take another look and reflect on the decision you are about to implement.

4. A mission statement is a living and dynamic document and should be the vanguard in your dealings with employees, vendors, and most of all, your customers!

Typical Mission Statement Might Read as Follows:

As a company, we exist to optimize the value that all our constituents, such as: stockholders, staff, customers, vendors and the communities in which we operate receive from being associated with us.

We Accomplish This By:

1. Creating open communication with our customers and business associates;

2. Ensuring that our vision and core values are understood and implemented at all times by all staff;

3. Actively managing our relationships to fairly balance the interests of all stakeholders; and,

4. Growing our business organically, by way of the development of new products and/or services.

Our Vision:

Our company is in the business of (State the Nature of Your Business Here) and we will grow and expand by serving our customers to the best of our ability. That means our staff and facilities are the only assets we possess. Extraordinary returns for our stockholders will be achieved when we develop value in our core businesses and when our company is a place where creative, productive people want to work. This can only be achieved by satisfying our customers. Our staff will want to work for our company because we trust them and recognize that, as long as we support them with training, education and facilities, they are capable of making most of the important decisions. We are structured to provide every member of our staff with the opportunity to grow, to own decisions and their results, to benefit from our mutual success, and to focus on satisfying the customers we serve.

We constantly strive to grow because we foster experimentation. We promote new ideas and create a management structure and work environment in which ideas can bubble up. Creative failure is recognized as a good thing because it leads to learning and learning leads to success.

Core Values

1. We are highly ethical (beyond merely complying with our legal obligations} in all dealings.

2. We believe in the worth of each member of our staff and that everyone is more productive and happy if they are given responsibility and authority to act.

3. Excellence is our primary competitive advantage. We will endeavor to ensure that excellence is achieved by our staff and for our customers.

4. We are committed to growth.

Decisions are best made:

5. By the people closest to the problem, the market, and the customer,

6. By people who are committed to a shared goal,

7. By those who have ownership in the results,

8. In a workplace where fun is not frowned upon, and

9. In an environment where a well-executed effort that doesn't work is preferred to not trying at all.

10. Certainly, more elements might be added to your statement, based on your collective vision of the company's overall goals and objectives.

Once a realistic agreement of mission is established, one that will meet the needs, interests, and desires of the company and those involved as a whole, then and only then should you embark on moving your venture forward — and hopefully it will not be a perilous one, but a fruitful and satisfying endeavor for everyone who has a stake in your company's success.

An Outline For Promotion

Promoting Yourself

1. Maintain a professional personal appearance.

2. Establish your business within the community where you live.

3. Join and become active in local business, civic, political, religious, and other professional or trade groups.

Promote Your Company

1. Understand clearly your company's purpose and objectives. Try personifying the company and writing "who" the company is in 25 words or less.

2. Develop a corporate image: logo, name of company, name of product. Select a company name that is short, sounds good, and needs to be heard only once or twice to be remembered.

3. Select a graphic image to support your product name and logo on business cards and stationary. The design should represent the business' purpose.

4. Make your employees aware that they represent your business, not only in written communications, but also over the telephone on sales calls, etc.

5. Make sure your customers know if you expand your product line or improve your product or service.

6. Examine how you are perceived in the market place. Create communications that will position yourself and your product in the front of the minds of the customers. Find out how your competition is perceived.

Promote Your Product or Service

1. Put together a short and long-range promotional plan, set your objectives and make the plan succinct, specific, measurable and realistic.

2. Evaluate results regularly. Drop or change anything that does not work.

3. When promoting, be creative: establish a theme, standardize your format, use one message, emphasize the benefits to your customers.

4. Read, keep your ears open, listen to people such as customers and learn from them.

5. Offer an equivalent item if an item you are currently selling becomes unavailable.

6. Back up your product or service with excellent customer service.

7. Participate or offer to speak at trade shows and conventions.

8. Form a customer focus group by bringing together a collection of people who are using your product or service. This will give your customers an open forum to discuss their needs and exchange ideas with others in the same field.

9. Send press releases about your new product or service to the local newspapers and trade magazines.

10. Use small give-aways such as calendars, notepads, pens, etc., anything that will keep your name and the name of your product or service in front of the person with whom you wish to deal.

Pricing Guidelines for Launching a New Product or Service

Based on the "Profit Impact of Marketing Strategy" (PIMS) Surveys, over 60% of all new products, which have a greater value (higher quality) relative to the competition, realized gains in market shares through their lifetime; while only about 40% of those products have lesser relative value (quality) and lesser quality through their lifetime result in market share gains.

Price, quality, service (timeliness) are the key elements in valuing any product or service. In the past, delivering two out of three was sufficient. Today customers expect all three!

Start-up companies and small businesses (during their "small" stage) tend to under price their products and services. The start-up entrepreneur often does not consider what it will take to multiply the sales of the product/service through a sales force or distribution and does not leave room in the price to cover these costs. If the under pricing is severe, undervaluing of the product and services in the eyes of the marketplace will hamper, if not prevent, the growth of the company into the goals desired.

Never sell on the basis of price. From the beginning, have your customers get used to VALUE and what your services or products do for them, so that you may always have some flexibility concerning price.

The key to pricing is to view your product or service through the eyes of your potential customers. Your bias is to find the highest value customers first, then increase your marketing efforts to them. Then you can achieve a premium price (statistically opting for the over 60% strategy listed above).

Achieving premium prices requires the identification of the high value customer, designing the product or service to match their higher value needs (improving the value)(increased quality, better functionality and in general doing more for the customer than their present choices). Decide how to reach that particular customer at the exclusion of the lower value customers in the market. The goal of the enterprise may be to ultimately serve lower value customers because of desired company size, but these customers likely cannot be served in the beginning of the enterprise, or introduction of the new product/service because of resources (human, financial, equipment, know-how, cost, etc.).

Select a price/quality strategy (economy, commodity (same as everyone else, good, average, better, or best) as the thrust of the product or service. Within whatever category of price/quality and customer definition, then determine some differential characteristics that can be offered that will result in your having a premium price within the confines of your strategy. In comparing yourself with the competition, be sure that you compare yourself first with competitors of like price/quality strategy. Competition with different price/quality (and possibly different delivery methods) are secondary competitors.

If we rate quality as "economy," "commodity," "good," "better," "best," the premium for best quality over economy is about 10%.

Do not price based on cost or on the competition. The goal is to price to the VALUE provided to customers within the constraints of not pricing below costs, and keeping in mind that the comparable value is your competitor's price (another constraint). You are looking for a competitive advantage in the design of your services and products and that should be worth something.

Pricing to "Meet The Competition" results in converting your products/services to commodities to match everyone else with no differentiation in other features/benefits. It is profitable only when you are already the low cost supplier and you can capture market share on other features/benefits.

If you MUST introduce a product/service at a lower price, then establish a promotion price and label it as such. Otherwise the penetration pricing strategy will backfire and your service or product will lose value - being established at the lower introductory price, and you never will be able to raise the price.

To use a price penetration strategy in order to gain market share (lower price than the value to the customer), the following usually have to be the case:

1. The market is price sensitive and will grow with small price reductions.
2. The market is growing in any event.
3. There is a strong after-market which you want to serve.
4. There is a SIGNIFICANT cost decrease with volume.
5. If you are already the low cost supplier and there is little price/value perception, keep the competition out.

Targeting margins or a defined return-on-sales in your marketing strategy means that there has to be money left on the table and therefore the value to the customer was more than the price you arbitrarily determined by some formula. This works when the market will take the volume at a higher price than you are offered, you are the market leader, the low cost supplier, and in high inflation.

Price can be used to position the product, creating an image or exclusivity. Cosmetics or other personal care products may be priced higher and achieve higher volume because you "treat yourself to the best" or "you are worth it." This strategy works when one of the following is the case: costs do not decrease with volume (providing a significant incentive to competition to get the higher volume for lower cost), you are the highest cost supplier, and you want to encourage competitive entry (rare).

The payoff for proper pricing and in serving the high value customer first will be to reduce the need for equity-financing at the beginning, and therefore conserve equity-value. For the entrepreneur, making a small amount of stock worth a significant amount in the future.

Patents, Copyrights, Trademarks, Servicemarks, and Trade Secrets

How do you protect your rights against others?

The following recommendations are offered as a means of protecting yourself from competitors, employees, consultants, suppliers, and other third parties.

Patents

Patents are granted for novel and unique inventions by the US Patent & Trademark Office (PTO) for 20 years from the date on which the application for the patent was filed in the United States or, if the application contains a specific reference to an earlier filed application under 35 U.S.C. 120, 121 or 365(c), from the date the earliest application was filed, and subject to the payment of maintenance fees as provided by law.

The paragraph (claims) at the end of the patent defines its scope. Ask your patent attorney what the claims in your competitor's patent or your patent cover; find out what others can do without infringing. Searches are extremely useful but not legally necessary. Additionally, a "patent pending" statement is not legally enforceable. Patents give the right to sue and to license others. Make certain a patent will help you in your business before spending big money on it and be prudent about infringing on your competitors' patents.

A maintenance fee is due 3 ½, 7 ½ and 11 ½ years after the original grant for all patents issued from the applications filed on and after December 12, 1980. The maintenance fee must be paid at the stipulated times to maintain the patent in force. After the patent has expired anyone may make, use, offer for sale or sell or import the invention without permission of the patentee, provided that matter covered by other unexpired patents is not used. The terms may be extended for certain pharmaceuticals and for certain circumstances as provided by law.

Copyrights

Copyrights are granted and protected for books, serials, recordings, movies, and videos by the US Library of Congress (LOC) in Washington, DC and are held for the life of the author plus 55 years and in the case of joint works the copyright continues for 55 years after the survivor's death. All "Intellectual Property Works" are protected by applying a notice at the time of first publication, and may be perfected by filing an application with the LOC.

In the case of works made for hire, the employer and not the employee is considered to be the author. Section 101 of the copyright law defines a "work made for hire" as: (1) a work prepared by an employee within the scope of his or her employment; or (2) a work specially ordered or commissioned for use as a contribution to a collective work, as a part of a motion picture or other audiovisual work, as a translation, as a supplementary work, as a compilation, as an instructional text, as a test, as answer material for a test, or as an atlas, if the parties expressly agree in a written instrument signed by them that the work shall be considered a work made for hire...

Copyrights are only protected in the form of an actually produced work, not the idea. Protectable works also include maps, music, paintings, computer programs, etc. If your work is international in scope, you may also want to register with the World Intellectual Property Organization (WIPO) in Geneva, Switzerland.

Trademarks & Servicemarks

A Trademark is either a word, phrase, symbol or design, or combination of words, phrases, symbols or designs, which identifies and distinguishes the source of the goods or services of one party from those of others. A Servicemark is the same as a trademark except that it identifies and distinguishes the source of a service rather than a product.

A trademark is different from a copyright or a patent. A copyright protects an original artistic or literary work; a patent protects an invention. You cannot reserve a trademark, because they arise only out of actual use. A search should be performed to assure that you are not using someone else's mark or something confusingly similar. Registration of the use of a trademark is of advantage both at the state and federal (PTO) level. Registration on a state level is made at your Secretary of State's office.

There are a number of legal firms and companies who specialize in patents, trademarks, and other intellectual property protection that will perform searches for you before you go through the process of registration. Companies such as Tompson & Tompson in Boston & Corsearch in New York can help with trademark searches and Rapid Patent in Arlington, VA can give you some help and direction in the complex arena of patents. However, do not overlook contacting the Library of Congress or the PTO yourself for preliminary information about the steps involved in the registration process and protection of your work. Information can also be gained by visiting their sites on the World Wide Web. The Library of Congress World Wide Web address is: http://www.loc.gov/ and the PTO can be found at: http://www.uspto.gov/.

Trade Secrets

Trade Secrets are information, not generally known, used in a business, protected against free disclosure, which give a competitive advantage. If someone, such as an employee or consultant takes this information by improper means, you may be able to legally enjoin its use. However, if someone finds the secret or secrets out independently, you cannot do anything about that.

So what can you do to protect yourself from someone pirating and using your trade secrets? You will probably want to consider having your attorney draw up two documents, which are generally known as "confidentiality" and "non-compete" agreements. These documents would and should be signed and dated by you and by your employees and vendors or other outsiders who would become knowledgeable about your trade secrets during the course of being in your employ or by doing business with you. These types of agreements can and will give you the upper hand in any litigation that may arise   as a result of   anyone pilfering and using your trade secrets to their advantage. (See Non-Compete & Non-Disclosure Sample Agreements)

A Typical Employee's Agreement Relating to Work Product, Confidential Information, Non-solicitation, and Inventions

AGREEMENT made this (Insert) day of (insert Month and Year) by and between (insert your company's name), (hereinafter shall be referred to as the "Company") and (Insert the name of the employee) (hereinafter shall be referred to as "Employee").

In consideration of his/her employment and the payment of compensation in the course of such employment by the Company, the Employee agrees to the following:

WORK PRODUCT

Any and all writings, systems, methods, ideas, and work products prepared, discovered or developed by the Employee during the period of his/her employment, which may be useful in or relate to any business activity of the Company, shall be fully disclosed in writing to an officer of the Company, and shall be the sole and exclusive property of the Company.

CONFIDENTIAL INFORMATION

Employee shall hold in a fiduciary capacity for the benefit of the Company all information, knowledge and data relating to or concerned with its operations, activities, sales, business and/or affairs, and Employee shall not, at any time hereafter, use, disclose or divulge any such information, knowledge or data to any person, firm or corporation other than to the Company or its designee(s) or except as may otherwise be required in connection with the business and affairs of the Company.

NON-SOLICITATION

Employee agrees that during the period of his/her employment hereunder, and for a further period of one year thereafter, he/she shall not, directly or indirectly:

1. Solicit, raid, entice or induce any employee of the Company or any of its subsidiaries or affiliates to be employed by any person, firm or corporation which is, directly or indirectly, in competition with the business or activities of the Company or any of its subsidiaries or affiliated companies: or

2. approach any such employee for these purposes; and/or

3. authorize or knowingly approve the taking of such action by other persons on behalf of any such person, firm or corporation in taking such action.

4. Solicit business from any of the Company's customers or prospects.

INVENTIONS

Employee shall promptly and fully communicate to the Company all inventions and improvements made or conceived by him/her (whether solely or in conjunction with others) during the term of his/her employment which:

1. are within the scope of the Company's then existing or contemplated business activities; or

2. result from, are suggested by, or are related to any research or investigation which is conducted by the Company.

3. Employee shall disclose to the Company each invention or improvement, which Employee believes, falls outside of paragraph 4 and any determination thereof, if in dispute, shall be settled by arbitration pursuant to paragraph 13 thereof.

Employee shall make and maintain adequate and current written records of all inventions and improvements within the scope of paragraph 4 in the form of notes, sketches, drawings or reports relating thereto, which records shall be and remain the property of, and be available to, the Company at all times.

Employee shall at any time during his/her or subsequent to his/her employment assist the Company or its nominees (at the Company's expense) to obtain patents for inventions and improvements within the scope of paragraph 4 in any and all countries, and shall give testimony and execute all papers for use in applying for, obtaining, sustaining and defending such patents.

All rights, title and interest to all inventions and improvements within the scope of paragraph 4, whether patented or not, shall be and remain the sole and exclusive property of the Company and its nominee.

Employee has attached hereto a complete list and brief description of all inventions and improvements, which he/she has made or conceived of prior to his/her employment by the Company, if any.

Employee shall notify the Company in writing before he/she makes any disclosure or performs or causes to be performed any work for or on behalf of the Company which conflicts or threatens to conflict with rights which he/she claims in connection with any invention of improvement contained in the list attached hereto, or. which conflicts or threatens to conflict with any other invention or improvement which is otherwise outside the scope of paragraph 14. If the Employee fails to give such notice to the Company, he/she shall not thereafter make claims against the Company with respect to the use of any such inventions or improvement in any work or the product of any work, which he/she performs or causes to be performed for or on behalf of the Company.

GENERAL

No waiver, amendment or modification of this Agreement shall be effective unless in writing and signed by both parties.

This Agreement shall be binding upon Employee, his/her heirs, executors and assignees and shall insure to the benefit of the Company, its successors and assignees.

Any controversy or claims arising out of or relating to this Agreement, or the breach thereof, shall be settled by: Arbitration in New York City in accordance with the Rules of the American Arbitration Association or may be entered in any court having jurisdiction.

Nothing in this agreement shall be deemed to restrict the Company's rights to terminate or change the employment of the Employee with or without cause. Termination of employment for whatever reason shall not release the Employee of any obligations incurred under this Agreement.

The terms "Company" as used in this Agreement shall include all present or future subsidiary corporations of (insert your company's name).

If any clause, paragraph, section or part of this agreement shall be held to be void, invalid, or illegal, for any reason, by any Court of competent jurisdiction, such provision shall be ineffective but shall not in any way invalidate or affect any other clause, paragraph, section or part of this agreement.

IN WITNESS WHEREOF, the parties hereto have executed the above Agreement and attached their respective seals as of the day and year first above written.

By: Employee _____ ___ Date: _____

_____
(Print or Type name of employee here)

By: _____ Date: _____

_____
(Print or type the name of the company representative here)

_____
For: (Insert the name of your company here)

Typical Non-Disclosure Agreement

This agreement, is between (insert the Name of Persons or Companies) collectively referred to hereafter as "You" et. al. on the one part and (insert the Name of Your Company) doing business as "The Name You Use to Conduct Business" on the other.

YOUR COMPANY NAME" anticipates the need to discuss with you(unannounced products, possible business relationships, marketing information, technological aspects of each other's organizations, features, services, et. al. in order to assist them in making business decisions concerning their respective interests in present and future business affiliations between the two organizations. In consideration of the mutual promises contained herein, and as a condition to the disclosure of information, "INSERT YOUR COMPANY NAME" and you agree as follows:

I.   This agreement shall become effective upon execution in writing by "INSERT YOUR COMPANY NAME" and You shall continue for a period of two (2) years unless sooner terminated in writing by both parties. You agree that all of your obligations undertaken herein with respect to confidential information received pursuant to this agreement.

II. INSERT YOUR COMPANY NAME" may, during the course of discussions, reveal to you certain confidential, proprietary and/or trade secret information concerning products, features, and services, some of which may not have been announced and are generally not available. Such information may include, without limitation, certain specifications, designs, plans, drawings, hard-ware, software, data, prototypes, or other business and technical information, which relate in whole or in part, to processors, office automation products, communications products or services and all related enhancements ("Confidential Information").All Confidential Information, in whatever form provided, shall remain the property of "INSERT YOUR COMPANY NAME".

III. For a period of three (3) years following the date of receipt of Confidential Information, you shall:
    A.   Not disclose such Confidential Information to third parties except:
    B.   those of your employees with a need to know and/or
    C.   those third parties for whom you have secured the prior written approval and
    D.   Advise employees who receive the Confidential Information of the existence of this agreement and of the confidentiality herein; and
    E.   Use and require your employees to use the utmost degree of care to protect the Confidential Information from improper disclosure.
    F.   Use the Confidential Information only for the purpose of assisting you in making business decisions concerning topics directly or indirectly to the substance of the discussions between the parties whether or not such discussions result in ongoing business associations for any length of time.

IV. Notwithstanding anything to the contrary herein, you shall have no obligation to preserve the confidentiality of any Confidential information which:
    A.   Prior to any disclosure by "INSERT YOUR COMPANY NAME" was known to you free of any obligation to keep confidential as evidenced by documentation in your possession; or
    B.   Is or becomes publicly available by other than unauthorized disclosure by you; or
    C.   Is developed by or on behalf of you Independent of any Confidential Information; or
    D.   Is received from a third party whose disclosure does not violate any confidentiality obligation.

V. Neither this Agreement or the disclosure or receipt of Confidential Information shall constitute or imply any promise or intention by you, to form, or expand, or otherwise change any business associations between "INSERT YOUR COMPANY NAME" and/or any other affiliate company, nor does this Agreement disclosure or receipt of Confidential information infer or commit to any purchase of products, features or services, or constitute or imply any promise, intention or commitment by "INSERT YOUR COMPANY NAME" with respect to the present or future marketing, sale, or pricing of the products, features or services or to furnish you with any Confidential Information.

VI.   Confidential Information furnished in written, pictorial, magnetic and/or other tangible form shall not be duplicated by you except as necessary for the purposes of this Agreement. You shall return all tangible Confidential Information (including copies, reproductions, or otherwise containing Confidential Information) within ten (10) business days to "INSERT YOUR COMPANY NAME" following a written request for same.

VII.   You agree that you shall not transmit, directly, or indirectly the Confidential Information received from "INSERT YOUR COMPANY NAME" thereunder, or any portion thereof, to any country outside the United States.

VIII.   Nothing contained in this Agreement shall be construed as granting or conferring upon you any rights by license or otherwise in any disclosed Confidential Information or under any trademark, patent, copyright or any other intellectual property right of "INSERT YOUR COMPANY NAME".

IX.   You agree not to announce or disclose to any third person or party your participation in discussions with "INSERT YOUR COMPANY NAME" concerning any unannounced product, feature, or service or the nature of any such discussions without first securing the prior written approval of "INSERT YOUR COMPANY NAME".

Your signature acknowledges that you have read and understand the terms and conditions set forth above.

IN WITNESS THEREOF, the undersigned parties have caused this Non-Disclosure Agreement to be executed by their respective duly authorized officers as of the date first written above.

By: _____

      (Signature)   (Print Name)

Title:_____

Company: _____Date:_____

By: _____

      (Signature)   (Print Name)

Title:_____

Company: _____ Date: _____

Time Management

First let me begin by saying, "No one can manage time, but what you can manage—is yourself!" So, from this viewpoint, just how can you make better use of the time you do have? Let me begin by paraphrasing one of the great professional football coaches of all time, Vince Lombardi who coached and brought the Green Bay Packers to six national championships during the 1960's who once said, "I have never lost a football game in my life, although I did run out of time on a few occasions. He also had a single theory for getting the job done...preparation, planning, and execution. Well the clock is ticking...so we had better get a move on!

The one entity that we all, at one time or another, have said we're running short of—is time. So, if you find that there are not enough hours in the day to do all that needs to be done, then I suggest that you begin by managing yourself a little better. Start by keeping a daily diary of your activities to find out how you use or misuse your time, and whether or not you're actually devoting your time to high priority projects, and I also suggest that you keep a record of the frequency and type of interruptions you deal with, for at least ten working days. This strategy should help you to identify and rid yourself of the culprits that are pilfering this most precious commodity...
your time.

The Following Are The Most Common Time Bandits

1. People interruptions — not to be confused with customer interruptions. A customer is not an interruption of work, but the reason for our work.

2. Telephone interruptions—the solicitor who wants to sell you a new phone system or copy machine.

3. Doing the work of employees...delegate, delegate, delegate!

Meetings that are unessential—believe it or not, but I once attended a meeting about holding a meeting... Frustrating??? To say the least!

4. Crisis management—Taking care of the urgent instead of the important.

5. Procrastination—waiting for others to take action... I am sure that you all may have known an individual or two who constantly exerted more time and energy looking for ways to avoid doing a task, in the hope that someone or something magical would happen to make the chore disappear, than it would have been to deal with the assignment in the first place...Do it and be done with it!

6. Lack of objectives, priorities, and deadlines—most important of these are "deadlines." Nothing is perceived as important unless it has a deadline connected to it!

How Do You Free Yourself of These Time Bandits?

1. Again, set deadlines. Have others check your progress. Reward yourself upon completion of difficult tasks.

2. Rank items on the basis of importance. Handle each item once.

3. Define policies and procedures. This eliminates the need for making routine decisions.

4. Again, learn to delegate. Stop doing the work of the employees. Insist they solve their own problems. People who are closest to the task should and are usually in a better position to make decisions as long as they understand that they share in the results.

5. Use the 80-20 rule. Identify and focus on the top 20% items, that make up 80% of the importance of your work.

6. Program recurring operations and decisions. Repetitive operations can be procedurized and accomplished by a clerk or computer.

7. Do unpleasant tasks first...get them out of the way and move on to something more palatable.

8. Do not procrastinate.

9. Keep yourself on schedule.

10. Escape for an hour or two each day to do some concentrated work in a place where you won't be interrupted.

    Maintain perspective: how does today's task relate to tomorrow's objective or your company's long-term mission, goals, and objectives?

11. Keep projects visible; they are more likely to get done that way. You know the old saying, "out of sight—out of mind."

How to Develop and Keep
A Solid Team of Employees

1. Hire lots of compulsive hard workers, and avoid well rounded types. Compulsive hard workers are different from workaholics who spend many hours on the job, but may not be particularity productive. Hard workers accomplish a lot because they focus their energy effectively. Work is not an escape for them...it's something they love to do.

2. Hire a few tigers. Then hire many dedicated workers who have reached their level of competence and know it. Put a few tigers in your tank. Channel their energies toward company goals rather than toward competition with each other. Then surround your tigers with a larger number of good, competent workers who know their job well and do it diligently...people who are not scrambling for promotions or grabbing at new career goals.

3. Keep the bandwagon rolling. High performers aren't lured by failure. Act like a winner. Be a manager with vision. Create an environment where accomplishment is amply rewarded.

4. Hire a few exceptionally creative people, then give them plenty of support. It doesn't take more than one or two highly creative people to generate all the ideas your company needs. But conceptualizers are often not practical doers. Be sure you have the staff support to turn ideas into workable, profitable projects.

5. Reward and encourage perseverance above all other virtues. People who demonstrate a willingness to press on even during the darkest hours should be hired and cultivated with enthusiasm because they can move mountains for the company.

6. Focus on leadership skills. Leadership is the quality in employees which supplies direction for other employees. Look for the quality of leadership in your employees and cultivate it.

7. Take a page from the Japanese Business Style handbook ...broaden your employees. Rotate a few of the most promising employees through different departments. Your future managers will need wide-ranging knowledge of the company. Breed a team of generalists, not specialists.

8. Remember the KISS formula: "KEEP IT SIMPLE STUPID." Probably the most dismal trend in management today is the compulsion to make things more difficult than they are.

9. Build on strengths rather than trying to correct weaknesses in people. Unearth those things that each employee can do best rather than those things that he or she can't do at all. Help your employees to build on their strengths.

Creating Enthusiasm in Your Workforce

Enthusiasm is perhaps the most important ingredient in establishing a positive performance attitude in any workforce. It makes you feel young and vibrant no matter what your age. It gives you energy that a less enthusiastic person lacks. Best of all, enthusiasm is contagious.

Listed below are fourteen ways to increase the enthusiasm in your company. These guidelines could help you increase your employees performance and your company's bottom line.

1. Objectives Must Be Clear

The way you state your corporate objectives may not relate well to individual staff members. It may be correct and to the point, and still not hit home. That does not mean it is wrong, it just means you must state it differently. People, on the average, need a simplistic goal or set of goals. It helps them focus and generates interest.

2. Lessons from Others

You can live the experiences yourself, or you can learn from others. The best way is to combine that which others have experienced with your own experiences. In doing so, you are in every sense of the word networking for success.

3. Self-image and Attitude

In Peter and Waterman's book, *In Search of Excellence*, they have a lot to say about winners. Most importantly is your own self-perception. Here is what they say:

"We all think we are tops. We're exuberantly, wildly irrational about ourselves. And that has sweeping implications for organizing. Yet most organizations, we find, take a negative view of their people. They verbally berate participants for poor performance. (Most actually talk tougher than they act,

but tough nonetheless intimidates people.) They call for risk-taking but punish even the tiny failures. They want innovation but kill the spirit of the champion. With their rationalist hats on, they design systems that seem calculated to tear down the workers' self-image. They might not mean to be doing that, but they are."

The message that comes through so poignantly in most studies reviewed, is that we like to think of ourselves as winners. The lesson that the excellent companies have to teach is that there is no reason why we can not design systems that continually reinforce this notion; most people feel that they are winners. Their populations are distributed around the normal curve, just like every other large population, but the difference is that their systems reinforce degrees of winning, rather than degrees of losing. Their people, by and large, reach their targets and quotas, because the targets and quotas are set (often by the people themselves) to allow that to happen.

4. Praise

Everyone likes to receive praise. It goes deeper than simply the desire to feel as though we are winners. We all need to feel appreciated. In their book *The One Minute Manager*, authors Blanchard and Johnson feel a manager should be praising people for doing things the right way. They should be praised for trying, where others might not have. Rather than constantly seeking out all the ills and problems, we should also devote ourselves to finding the things that are right, then make sure they happen again.

5. Celebration

In the book *Corporate Cultures*, authors Deal and Kennedy refer to these celebrations as ceremonies. They state: *"Whether they are cultural extravaganzas or simple events when employees pass particular milestones, ceremonies help the company celebrate heroes, myths, and sacred symbols. Like habits rituals are commonplace and taken for granted. Ceremonies, meanwhile, are extraordinary; the full corporate spotlight shines on them. Ceremonies place the culture on display and provide experiences that are remembered by employees."*

6. Simplicity & Complexity

In developing your program, it is essential to keep information simple and easily understandable. Although in reality it will be a rather involved and somewhat complex strategy, that fact can never be revealed to the masses. They must perceive the program as spontaneous, to some degree, and simple in form.

7. Action

Every action you take must be pointed in the direction of achieving the overall goal. That means every manager must be fully behind this motivational program in action as well as word. The worst thing that could happen concerning your desire to motivate your people is for the various departments to take different courses of action.

Also, the program must be designed in such a manner as to get the employees to act in the way you would like them to act. If we believe that we are what we do, then these actions are very important. You must expect some failures. The important thing is that the action occurs. In a very short time those failures will be turned into a multiplicity of success.

8. Heroes

Every culture has its heroes or heroines. It's important for people to admire others so that they can mirror their actions. We all have gained something from our own heroes, who could have been one of our own parents, a teacher, a sports figure, an entertainer, or a friend. Corporations must strive to offer enough genuine "good" heroes. Any large, or for that matter, small organization has the ability to create heroes...good solid role models.

9. Self-determination

People like to feel as if they determine the events that affect their lives. In fact, it is an important aspect of success for people to take responsibility for their own lives. While it is important for a company to supply financial security, it would be a mistake to shield them from the realities of business. If things are going poorly, they should be told, offered solutions and asked for their input.

In your plan, it will be important to devise methods for communicating to the employees on a regular schedule. These methods should provide a base of information that is accurate and informative. Through these and other types of communication, you should elicit responses from the employees. If you ask for their input, they will feel like they have more control over their own destiny.

10. Structure

In reviewing the previous materials, I believe it is essential to develop a structure that rewards everyone to some degree. After all, there are degrees of success within every job. And remember, everyone thinks he or she is a winner. You will get a lot more out of your people if they believe they are winners, at least to some degree.

Remember: The structure of your program should be unseen to be most effective. It should appear to be a natural part of the way things are done.

11. Symbols

We all need symbols of recognition, things we can display or show others. It's great to be told you are doing well, but it is even better to also receive a symbol of your success. In the case of the formal events, these symbols should have a substantial value. They should say to everyone who sees them that the owner of one of these prestigious awards has made an important contribution to the company. As for the informal awards, they could simply be represented by a plaque, a certificate, or some token of your appreciation. One thing to remember is that no award large or small is meaningful if it is given without feeling.

12. Long-term Strategy

A successful motivational program will require long-term planning. My suggestion is that you make your motivational program part of the strategic planning process. It can be molded and shaped to fit the changing business and personal environments that affect our thinking.

13. Yearly Campaign & Themes

The creation of themes is very important to the communication process. Themes are memorable and should have a message that is readily identifiable with the corporate objectives. For example, you might want your management team to be more aggressive, develop a fighting attitude, and have a more competitive spirit. A good theme for this would be "The Eye of The Tiger," "Dream the Impossible Dream" or for a specified period of time the message to the employees should revolve around the theme. Every chance you get reinforce the concept of the theme do so.

14. Communication Process

There are formal and informal communications. The formal communication process includes all those things you use to inform the employee base with: advertising, memos, publications, meetings, etc. informal communications comes from gossip, reading between the lines, rumors, and most importantly, the actions of management. It's easy to control the formal communications process but very difficult to do the same with the informal process. It is important to get control of the informal process because it is generally the stronger of the two. Somehow we tend to believe the rumors and gossip before we believe what we are told by our leaders. Of course, there is some information that cannot be openly discussed, but when possible, sharing the truth, good or bad, will increase credibility and defuse the rumor bomb before it explodes.

As managers, you must learn methods of communicating that will help people achieve motivation. It is becoming more apparent that a good manager must add to his or her skills the ability to work well with people.

Employment Rights, Wrongful Discharge, and Sexual Harassment

While many states recognize employees' claims of wrongful discharge and the importance of employment stability, the law is grounded in the doctrine of employment "at-will." This means that an employer, absent a contract or a specific statutory prohibition, generally retains the right to promote, terminate, hire, and set the compensation of employees as it sees fit.

Here Are 8 Simple Do's & Don'ts For Employers:

1. Do not impose different requirements or offer different pay to employees or prospective employees based upon their race, sex, age, creed, national origin, handicap, religion, sexual orientation or other individual characteristics protected by federal law or the governing laws of your state.

2. Do not request that anyone take a physical examination before you have given a prospective employee a firm offer of employment.

3. Do not target a particular group of employees based upon age or other characteristics in the event of a reduction in your workforce.

4. Do not use age, race, gender, sexual orientation, or handicap as a determining factor in any employment decision.

5. Do not passively yield to a hostile work environment by permitting your workers to create an atmosphere that can be offensive and by all means take steps to curb any such behavior.

6. Develop and articulate clear company policies relating to discipline, advancement, or discharge and fulfill those policies in a fair and equitable manner.

7. Train everyone in a supervisory capacity to fairly apply your company's policies to all employees equally. And, by all means, do not let your supervisors practice favoritism, as well as cautioning them to avoid the appearance of doing anything that can be interpreted as favoritism.

8. If the state in which you do business has a "Family Medical Leave Act" or other laws governing employment practices not mentioned here, make sure you acquire such documentation from your local State Labor Board or other governing body where your business is located ...Need I say more?

Positioning Products & Services

Positioning is a concept that has changed the landscape of advertising. A concept so simple some people have a great deal of difficulty understanding just how powerful it is.

What is Positioning?

Positioning originates with a product, service, company, institution, or even a person (a politician or celebrity for example). However, positioning is not what you do to a product, but what you do to the mind of the prospective buyer. So, it is really inaccurate to call the concept "product positioning" as if you were doing something special to the product itself. Not that positioning doesn't involve change. It does. But changes made in the name, the price and the package are really not changes in the product at all. They are fundamentally cosmetic changes done for the purpose of securing a worthwhile position in the prospects mind. Positioning is also the central idea that addresses the problems of getting heard in our over-communicated society.

How Did the Concept of Positioning Get Started?

If one word can be used to describe the direction of advertising over the last thirty years, that word would be "positioning." Slogans such as: "We're the third largest selling coffee in America." say the Sanka people. The third largest? What became of words like "first," "best," and "finest?" Well, the so called "good old days of advertising" are gone forever and so is some of the vocabulary. In today's marketplace you find comparatives not superlatives. "Avis is only No. 2 in rent-a-cars, so why go with us? We try harder." Which, was one of the most successful advertising campaigns of its day—it endured successfully for about twelve years." "Seven-up: the un-cola" also rode on the crest of a wave for years. In the advertising world, these statements are called positioning slogans. And the advertising people who write them spend their time and research money looking for positions, or holes to fill, in the marketplace. Moreover, positioning has created interest well beyond the Madison Avenue crowd and with good reason. Because just about anyone can use positioning strategy to get ahead in life. And if you do not understand and use these principals, your competition assuredly will.

Just What Is Positioning All About?

How did a hard-sell concept like positioning become so popular in a business noted for its creativity? In truth, the past two decades might appropriately be characterized as a "return to reality." White knights and black eye patches gave way to such positioning concepts as Lite Beer is, "Everything you have always wanted in a great beer--And Less." Poetic? Yes. Artful? Yes. But also a straightforward, clearly defined explanation of the basic positioning premise. To be successful today, you must touch base with reality. And the reality that really counts is what's already in the prospect's mind. To be creative, to create something that doesn't already exist in the mind, is becoming more and more difficult If not impossible. The basic approach of positioning is not to create something new and different but, to manipulate what's already up there in the mind. To retie the connections that already exist. Today's marketplace is no longer responsive to the strategies that worked in the past. There are just too many products, too many companies, and too much marketing noise.

The Overcommunicated Society

In today's marketplace we have become an over-com-municated society. The per-capita consumption of advertising in America today is about $200 a year. If you spend $1 million a year on advertising, you are bombarding the average consumer with less than a half-cent of advertising, spread out over 365 days. A consumer already exposed to $200 worth of advertising from other companies. In our overcomm-unicated society, to talk about the impact of your advertising is to seriously over-state the potential effectiveness of your message. It is an egocentric view that bears no relationship to the realities of the marketplace. In the communication jungle out there the only hope to score big is to be selective, to concentrate on narrow targets, to practice segmentation. In a word, "positioning." The mind, as a defense against the volume of today's communications, screens and rejects much of the information offered it. In general, the mind accepts only that which matches prior knowledge or experience.

Millions of dollars have been wasted trying to change minds with advertising. Once a mind is made up, it's almost impossible to change it. Certainly not with a weak force like advertising. "Do not confuse me with the facts, my mind is made up." That's a way of life for most people.

The average person can tolerate being told something which he or she knows nothing about (Which is why "news" is an effective advertising approach.) But, the average person cannot tolerate being told he or she is wrong therefore, mind-changing is the road to advertising disaster.

The Oversimplified Message

The best approach to take in our overcommunicated society is the oversimplified message. In communication, as in architecture, less is more. You have to sharpen your message to cut into the mind. You have to jettison the ambiguities, simplify the message, and then simplify it some more if you want to make a long-lasting impression. People who depend on communication for their livelihood know the necessity of over simplification. Let us say you are meeting with a politician whom you are trying to get elected. In the first five minutes you will learn more about your political product than the average voter is going to learn in the next five years. Since so little material about your candidate is ever going to get into the mind of the voter, your job is really not a "communication" project in the ordinary meaning of the word. It is a selection project. You have to select the material that has the best chance of getting through. The enemy that is keeping your messages from hitting pay dirt is the volume of communication. Only when you appreciate the nature of the problem can you understand the solution.

71

When you want to communicate the advantages of a political candidate or a product or even yourself, you must turn things inside out. You look for the solution to your problem not inside the product, not even inside your own mind. You look for the solution to your problem inside the prospect's mind. In other words, since so little of your message is going to get through anyway, you ignore the sending side and concentrate on the receiving end. You concentrate on the perceptions of the prospect, not the reality of the product. In politics says John Lindsay, "the perception is the reality" so, too, in advertising, in business and in life. But what about truth? What about the facts of the situation? Every human being seems to believe intuitively that he or she alone holds the key to universal truth. When we talk about truth, what truth are we talking about? The view from the inside or the view from the outside? It does make a difference. In the words of another era, "The customer is always right." And by extension the seller is always wrong. It may seem cynical to accept the premise that the sender is wrong and the receiver is right, but you really have no other choice. Not if you want to get your message accepted by another human mind. Besides, who's to say that the view from the inside looking out is any more accurate than the view from the outside looking in? By turning the process around, by focusing on the prospect rather than the product, you simplify the selection process. You also learn principles and concepts that can greatly increase your communication effectiveness.

The Oversimplified Mind

The only defense a person has in our over-communicated society is an oversimplified mind, Not unless they repeal the law of nature that gives us only 24 hours in a day will they find a way to stuff more into the mind. The average mind is already a dripping sponge that can only soak up more information at the expense of what is already there, Yet we continue to pour more information into that supersaturated sponge and are disappointed when our messages fail to get through. Advertising, of course, is only the tip of the communication iceberg. We communicate with each other in a wide variety of bewildering ways, and in a geometrically increasing volume. The medium may not be the message, but it does seriously affect the message. Instead of a transmission system, the medium acts like a filter. Only a tiny fraction of the original material ends up in the mind of the receiver. Furthermore, what we receive is influenced by the nature of our over-communicated society. "Glittering generalities" have become a way of life in our over-communicated society -- not to mention that they work.

Technically, we are capable of increasing the volume of communication at least tenfold. Already there is direct television broadcasting from satellites. Every home would have over 60 channels or so to choose from. And there's more to come. Texas Instruments has announced a "magnetic bubble" memory device that can store 92,000 bits of information on a single chip. Six times as much as the largest semiconductor memory device now on the market. Terrific! But who is working on a magnetic bubble for the mind? Who is trying to help the prospect cope with the complexity that so overwhelms the mind that the average reaction to the wealth of information today is to tighten the intake valve? To accept less and less of what is so freely available? Communication itself is the communication problem.

Recommendations About Advertising

What Is A Good Advertisement?

There are several schools of thought about this subject. Some advertising agencies hold that a good advertisement is an advertisement with the clients OK on it. Another school accepts the definition, which holds that a good advertisement is one that sells a product without drawing attention to itself. For example: Instead of having a reader say, "What a clever advertisement," the reader says, "I never knew that before. I must try this product." The recommendations listed below are based on several sources of research:

A. The experience of mail order advertisers puts them in a better position to measure the results of every advertisement they write. Their view is not obscured by those complex channels of distribution that make it impossible for most companies to dissect the results of their ads from all other factors in their marketing mix. The mail order advertiser has no retail stores to shrink and expand inventories, to push his product or to hide it under the counter. They must rely on their advertisements to do the entire selling job.

B. Another most valuable source of information is the experience of department stores. They depend on information gathered by research gathered by several companies such as Gallop, Starch, and others for insight about what makes people read advertisements and more importantly, the factors that make people remember what they read.

C. The tremendous amount of scientific research that's been done and continues to be done in broadcast.

D. Finally, being an observant student and brain picker of your predecessors and competitors.

Here are some recommendations:

1. What you say is more important than how you say it. What really motivates consumers to buy or not to buy is the content of your advertising, not its form. Your most important job is to decide what your are going to say about your product, and what benefit you promise.

2. Build your campaign around a great idea.

3. Give the facts. Very few advertisements contain enough factual information to sell the product

4. You cannot bore people into buying. The average family is now exposed to more than 1500 advertisements a day. The average woman now reads only four of the advertisements that appear in magazines.

5. Be well mannered, but do not clown. People do not buy from bad mannered salespeople; and research has shown that they do not buy from bad mannered advertisements. You should try to charm the consumer into buying your product.

6. Make your advertisement contemporary.

7. If you are lucky enough to write a good advertisement, repeat it until it stops pulling. You are not advertising to a standing army; you are advertising to a moving parade.

8. Do not lie. You wouldn't tell lies to your family. Do not tell them to mine. If you do not think the product is good, you should not be advertising it.

9. Image & Identification. How do you decide what kind of image to build? There is no short answer. Research cannot help you here. You've got to use judgment.

Most companies are reluctant to accept any limitation when it comes to their image. They want to be all things to all people, thus winding up with a wishy-washy personality or no image at all. Ninety-five percent of all ads in circulation right now are being created without any reference to long term considerations. They are being created ad hoc. Hence the lack of any consistent image from one ad to another or, even worse, one year to another. It takes uncommon guts to stick to one style in the face of all the pressures to come up with something new." It is tragically easy to be stampeded into change. However, golden rewards await the advertiser who has the brains to create a coherent image, and the stability to stick with it over a long period.

Most companies who find it expedient to change their image, want it changed upward. Often it has acquired a bargain-basement image, a useful asset in times of economic scarcity, but a grave embarrassment in the better days, when the majority of consumers are on their way up the social ladder.

The company that dedicates its advertising to building the most sharply defined image for itself will get the largest share of the market and the highest profits.

"Price Off "deals and other such hypodermics find favor with sales managers, but their effect is ephemeral, and they can be habit forming. Promotions cannot produce more than a temporary kink in the sales curve. A steady diet of price-off promotions lowers the esteem in which the consumer holds the product. Can anything that is always sold at a discount be desirable?

Do not be a copycat. If you have the good fortune to create a good campaign you will soon see others stealing it. This is irritating, but do not let it worry you; nobody has ever built a business by imitating someone else's advertising. Imitation may be the sincerest form of plagiarism, but it is also the mark of an inferior person.

How To Write Potent Copy
For Print, Television & Radio

Headlines:

1. The headline is the ticket on the meat. It is the most important element in most advertisements. It's the telegram that makes the reader decide whether to read the copy or not. Use it to flag down the readers who are prospects for the kind of product you are advertising. If you are selling a remedy for bladder weakness, display the words Bladder Weakness in your headline; they catch the eye of everyone who suffers from this inconvenience. If you want mothers to read your advertisement, display mothers in your headline, and so on.

2. Every headline should appeal to the reader's self-interest. It should promise a benefit.

3. Always try to inject news into your headlines, because the consumer is always on the lookout for new products, or new ways to use an old product, or new improvements in an old product. The two most powerful words you can use in a headline are Free & New. You can seldom use Free, but you can almost always use new - if you try hard enough.

4. Other words and phrases which work wonders are: How-To, Suddenly, Now, Announcing, Introducing, It's Here, Just Arrived, Important Development, Amazing, Sensational, Remarkable, Revolutionary, Startling, Miracle, Magic, Offer, Quick, Easy, Wanted, Challenge, Advise To, The Truth About, Compare, Bargain, Hurry, Last Chance etc.. Do not turn your nose up at these clichés. They may be shopworn but they work. That's why you see them turn up so often in the headlines of mail-order advertisers and others who can measure

79

the results of their advertisements. Headlines can be strengthened by the inclusion of emotional words, like Darling, Love, Fear, Proud, Friend, and Baby.

5. Five times as many people read the headline as read the body copy, so it is important that these glances should at least be told what brand is being advertised. Always include the brand name in your headlines.

6. Include your selling promise in your headline. This requires long headlines. Headlines often words or longer, containing news and information, consistently sold more merchandise than short headlines. Headlines containing six to twelve words pull more coupon returns than short headlines.

7. People are more likely to read your body copy if your headline arouses their curiosity; so you should end your headline with a lure to read on..

8. Some copywriters write tricky headlines, puns, literary allusions, and other obscurities that do not make sense to anyone but the author. This is, in many cases, an insult to both the client and the audience. In the average newspaper, your headline has to compete for attention with 350 others. Research has shown that readers travel so fast through this jungle that they do not stop to decipher the meaning of obscure headlines. Your headline must telegraph what you want to say, and it must telegraph it in plain language. Do not play games with the reader.

9. Research shows that it is dangerous to use negatives in headlines. If, for example, you write OUR SALT CONTAINS NO ARSENIC, many readers will miss the negative and go away with the impression that you wrote OUR SALT CONTAINS ARSENIC.

10. Avoid blind headlines--the kind which mean nothing unless you read the body copy underneath them, most people do not.

Body Copy:

When you sit down to write body copy, pretend you are talking to someone at a dinner party. They just asked you, "I'm thinking of buying a new car. Which would you recommend?" Write your copy as if you were answering that type of question.

1. Do not beat about the bush - get straight to the point.

2. Avoid superlatives, generalizations, and platitudes. Be specific and factual. Be enthusiastic, friendly, and memorable. Do not be a bore. There is a universal belief in lay circles that people won't read long copy. Nothing could be farther from the truth. There's a tale about an advertising copywriter who once wrote five pages of solid text for a beer company, moved it up from fifth to first place within about six months. Every advertisement should be a complete sales pitch for your product. It is unrealistic to assume that consumers will read a series of advertisements for the same product. So, do not be afraid to shoot for the works in every advertisement, on the assumption that it is the only chance you will ever have to sell your product to your prospect—it's now or never.

3. The more you tell - the more you sell.

4. If possible, include testimonials in your copy. The reader finds it easier to believe the endorsement of a fellow consumer than the fluffery of an anonymous copywriter. Every type of advertiser has the same problem: namely to be believed. Testimonials from celebrities get remarkably high attention. The better known the celebrity, the more attention you will attract. Occasionally you can cast your entire copy in the form of a testimonial.

5. Another profitable approach is to give your audience helpful advice, or service. It hooks about 75% more attention than copy that deals strictly with the product.

6. Avoid oratory "The priceless ingredient of every product is its honor and integrity." David Ogilvy, of the Ogilvy & Mather Advertising Agency, was once quoted, "When a company boasts about its integrity, or a woman about her virtue, avoid the former and cultivate the latter."

7. Unless you have some special reason to be solemn and pretentious, write your copy in a familiar language style that your customers use in everyday conversation.

8. Resist the temptation to write the kind of copy that wins awards. Most awards are the "Kiss of Death." Nearly all campaigns that produce results never win awards.

9. Avoid the temptation to entertain. This can be a recklessly sensitive area—something that is very funny to you, may be extremely offensive to others so, be careful.

Illustrations

1. The subject of your illustration is more important than its technique. As in all forms of advertising, substance is more important than form.

2. Gallup research has discovered that the kind of photographs which win awards from camera clubs--sensitive, subtle, and beautifully composed--do not work in advertisements.

3. What does work are photographs which arouse the readers interest and curiosity. If you take the trouble to get great photographs for your advertisements you will sell more. Before and after photographs seem to fascinate readers and viewers, and to make their point better than

any words. So does a challenge to the reader to tell the difference between two similar photographs.

4. The cast of characters in most people's dreams contains more people of their own sex than of the opposite sex. When you use a photograph of a woman, men ignore your advertisement and visa versa.

5. Advertisements are twice as memorable, on average, when they are illustrated in color. Avoid historical subjects. They may be useful for advertising whiskey, but for nothing else.

6. Do not show enlarged close-ups of the human face; they seem to repel readers. keep your illustrations as simple as possible, with the focus on one or two people, crowd scenes do not pull.

7. Whenever possible, avoid stereotyped situations like grinning housewives pointing to open refrigerators.

8. Showing owners faces is a better strategy than it may sound, because the public is more interested in personalities, than in companies.

Layout

Always design your layout for the publication in which it will appear, and never approve it until you have seen a proof copy and how it looks when pasted in that publication.

A layout must relate to the graphic climate of the newspaper or magazine which is to carry it. There is no need for an advertisement to look like an advertisement. If you make them look like editorial pages, you will attract 50% more readers. You might think the public would resent this trick, but there is no evidence to suggest they do. Magazine editors have discovered that people read the captions under photographs more than They read the text of their articles: and the same thing is true of advertisements. Research has shown, twice as many people read captions as read the body copy. It follows that you should never use a photograph without putting a caption under it, and each caption should be a sales pitch in miniature, complete with brand name and promise.

If you need long copy, there are several devices that are known to increase readership:

1. A display subhead of two or three lines, between your headline and your body copy, will heighten the reader's appetite for the feast to come.

2. If you start your body copy with a large initial letter, you will increase readership by an average of 13 per cent

3. Keep your opening paragraph down to a maximum of eleven words. A long first paragraph frightens readers away. All your paragraphs should be as short as possible; long paragraphs are fatiguing.

4. After two or three inches of copy, insert your first cross-head, and thereafter pepper cross-heads throughout They keep the reader marching forward. Make some of them interrogative, to excite curiosity in the next run of copy. An ingenious sequence of boldly displayed cross-heads can deliver the substance of your entire pitch to glancers who are too lazy to wade through text.

5. Set your copy in columns not more than forty characters wide. Most people acquire their reading habits from newspapers so use columns of about twenty-six characters. The wider the measure, the fewer the readers.

6. Type smaller than 9-point is difficult for most people to read.

7. Serif type, such as seen here, is easier to read than sans serif type seen here.

8. "Widows" increase readership. Except at the bottom of a column, where they make it too easy for the reader to quit.

9. Break up the monotony of long copy by setting key paragraphs in **boldface** or *italic*.

10. Insert illustrations from time to time, when appropriate.

11. Help the reader into your paragraphs with arrowheads, bullets, asterisks, and marginal marks.

12. If you have many unrelated facts to recite, do not try to relate them with cumbersome connectives; simply number them.

13. Never set your copy in reverse (white type on a black background), and never set it over a gray or colored tint. These devices, sometimes make reading physically impossible.

14. If you use leading between paragraphs, (an extra line space) you increase readership by an average of 12%.

15. The more typographical changes you make in your headline, the fewer people will read it. It is recommended that you run straight through your headlines in the same typeface, in the same size, and in the same weight.

16. Set your headline, and indeed your whole advertisement, in lower case. Capital letters are much harder to read, probably because we learn to read in lower case. People read all their books, newspapers, and magazines in lower case.

17. Never deface your illustration by printing your headline over it. Old-fashioned art directors love doing this, but it reduces the attention value of the advertisement by an average of 19%. Newspaper editors never do it. In

general, imitate the editors, they form the reading habits of your customers.

18. When your advertisement is to contain a coupon, and you want the maximum returns, put it at the top, bang in the middle. This position pulls 80% more coupons than the traditional outside-bottom of the page.

19. Make all your layouts project a feeling of good taste, provided that you do it unobtrusively. An ugly layout suggests an ugly product. Very few products do not benefit from being given a first-class ticket through life. In a socially mobile society, people do not like to be seen consuming products that their friends regard as second-class.

Television

The most valuable source of information is the factor analyses from Mapes & Ross, a company that measure changes in brand preference. People who register a change in brand preference after seeing a commercial subsequently buy the product three times more than people who do not. Research organizations also measure the recall of commercials, and this method finds favor with many advertisers. However, some commercials which get high recall scores get low scores on changing brand preference, and there appears there appears to be no correlation between recall and purchasing. I prefer to rely on changes in brand preference.

The following are the ten best types of commercials that are found to be above average in their ability to change people's brand preference:

1. Humor - Conventional wisdom has always held that people buy products because they believe them to be nutritious, or labor-saving, or a good value for the money - not because the manufacturer tells jokes on television. But, the latest wave of factor-analyses reveals that humor can now sell. (This doesn't mean you should be a clown.)

2. Slice of life - these playlets have been successful in case after case.

3. Testimonials-The most effective testimonial commercials are those which show loyal users of your product testifying to its virtues - when they do not know they are being filmed. When you pick loyal users, avoid those who would give such polished performances that viewers would think they were professional actors.

4. Demonstrations - which show how well your product performs are above average in their ability to persuade, Demonstrations do not have to be dull.

5. Problem/solution - This technique is as old as television. You show the viewer a problem with which he or she is familiar, and then show how your product can solve it.

6. Spokesperson. - This is the name given to commercials which consist of a distinguished pitch man or woman extolling the virtues of a product People find them non-creative, and are sick of them, but several advertisers still use them because they are above average in changing brand preference.

7. Characters - In some commercials, a *character* is used to sell your product over a period of years. The character becomes the living symbol of the product

8. Reason why - Commercials which give the viewer a rational reason why they should buy your product are slightly above average.

9. News - Commercials which contain news are above average. But even when they have news to tell, it is often underplayed or left out altogether.

10. Emotion - Researchers have not yet found a way to quantify the effectiveness of emotion but commercials with a large content of nostalgia, charm and even sentimentality can be enormously effective.

Radio

1. Identify your product or service early in the commercial and identify it often.

2. Promise the listener a benefit early in the commercial and repeat it often.

3. If at all possible, think about a specific music track or jingle can be developed into a theme song that could be used to identify the product, service, or the name of your company or business...the message can be changed often but, the jingle or music will become the recognizable and become a memorable messenger, such as UPS also known as Brown.

4. If you are trying to reach a male audience...use a male voice in your commercial, if your want to reach a female audience...use a female voice. if you want to reach both...use both. Studies have shown this approach works more favorably, as a male voice tends to attract male listeners and a female voice tends to attract female listeners, children attract other children, parents & grandparents etc.

More About Advertising

Strategy for Gain

The greatest area of concern and importance in the marketing and selling plan of a business lies in the formulation of an advertising budget. Most companies continue to regard advertising as a cost - in some cases, as money that could be better spent. Yet, research has shown that when a buyer is exposed to advertising prior to the sale, dollar sales can increase by up to 20%. You need to reach your buying public.

Your Objectives

Clear and measurable objectives must be established before   any funds are committed to an advertising effort. It's not enough to set goals of "increased sales" or to make consumers "aware" of your product or service. Objectives must be specific. Your objectives may be the creation of a new customer base; the increased or extended usage of your product; increased amount of product purchased; or promoting frequent replacement and/or maintenance. Other objectives might be to aid distributors; improve brand name recognition; or, create new sales leads. Once you have specified what goals and objectives you want to achieve you can begin working on formulating and defining your advertising budget.

Your Budget

Administrators, presidents, CEO's and their management teams must realize that advertising costs include not only media exposure but can include marketing and media research, creative services, sales training, and agency fees. In addition, there are trade show exhibits, sales literature, catalogues, brochures, and public relations efforts.

Several methods can be used in formulating an advertising budget. Each of these methods though useful in its own way carries major flaws. There is the competitive method, percentage of sales method, and historical method. There is also a fixed sum method, an affordable method, the profit margin method, and sales force vis-à-vis advertising method.

The most effective and least risky method to use in formulating a successful and profitable advertising budget is the *budget by objective* method. This method helps you allocate funds accordingly, to attain your specific and measurable goals.

To begin, follow these five simple steps.

1. Set specific, realistic, & measurable marketing objectives.

2. Plan activities that will meet the needs of these objectives.

3. Total the expenditures needed for every portion of your advertising plan.

4. Include a reserve for maintenance costs.

5. Your final advertising budget should be the result of total expenditures plus the maintenance reserve.

The most difficult part of this process will be estimating the effort needed to achieve your objectives. However, this can be overcome through experience and measured productivity. Systematic testing of results at varying budget levels can also be helpful in determining the required effort.

In addition, certain rules of thumb can aid you in formulating your advertising budget:

1. When the product or service is a high-volume, high-margin, or an impulse-purchase item where advertising will have a significant impact on your sales, allocate no less than 8% to 15% of total revenues for advertising.

2. When the product or service has a large average invoice, is a pre-planned purchase and has a profit margin ranging from 25% to 50%, allocate no less than 5% to 8% of revenue for advertising.

3. 3% to 7% of revenue should be allocated for sales of commercial and/or industrial products.

When formulating your advertising budget, it is important to remember that advertising is a profitable investment. Advertising leads to higher sales. Not only should your advertising budget be considered a fixed expenditure, but flexibility should remain for budget adjustment, maintenance costs, and media cost increases.

To ensure that the right strategy is developed for the right market every advertising dollar must be carefully spent. An advertising budget reflects a marketing philosophy and, as studies have shown, companies that aggressively advertise are likely to be more aggressive in other business attitudes, as well. Maintain an aggressive advertising attitude and you will strengthen your market share and sales position.

Average Advertising Investments

Compiled from 23 retail business organization sources by the Newspaper Advertising Bureau, Inc.

This Information is Broken Down by Business Type and Percentage of Gross Sales for Advertising

Appliances, TV & Stereo ----------------------------------- 2.3%

Auto Parts & Accessory ------------------------------------ 0.9%

Auto Dealers -- 0.8%

Bakeries --- 0.7%

Banks, Commercial -- 1.3%

Book Stores -- 1.7%

Camera & Photo Supply ------------------------------------- 2.4%

Children & Infant Wear ------------------------------------- 1.4%

Cocktail Lounges -- 0.9%

Department Stores --- 2.6%

Discount Stores -- 2.4%

Drug Stores -- 1.5%

Dry Cleaners --- 1.7%

Family Clothing -- 1.5%

Farm Equipment Dealers ------------------------------------ 0.6%

Floor Covering --- 1.8%

Florists --- 2.1%

Food Chains -- 1.1%

Furniture Stores --- 5.5%

Gasoline Stations -- 2.1%

Gift & Novelty -- 1.2%

Hair Stylist Male or Female ------------------------------- 2.0%

Hardware Stores --- 1.7%

Hotels-- 6.7%

Insurance Agents-- 1.8%

Jewelry Stores -- 4.4%

Liquor Stores -- 0.9%

Lumber Dealers -- 0.7%

Men's Stores & Schools------------------------------------ 2.8%

Music Stores -- 1.8%

Office Supply & Equipment Stores------------------------ 1.0%

Paint & Wallpaper Stores --------------------------------- 1.3%

Professional Services - Doctors/Lawyers/etc. ---------- 3.1%

Real Estate Developers ------------------------------------ 1.3%

Restaurants -- 1.8%

Saving & Loan/Mortgage Co.s ---------------------------- 1.5%

Shoe Stores --- 2.0%

Sporting Goods Stores-------------------------------------- 3.5%

Supermarkets--- 1.1%

Tire Stores --- 2.2%

Taverns-- 0.7%

Travel Agents -- 5.0%

Variety Stores--- 1.2%

Women's Wear Stores -------------------------------------- 3.0%

Annual Marketing Budget Worksheet

      The following is an example of an annual budget worksheet that can be used to formulate an annual budget:

Previous Year's Gross Annual Volume ....$_____

Projected Volume for Planned Year ....$_____

Percentage of Gross Volume for Marketing .... _____%

Projected Total Annual Budget for Marketing ....$_____

Planned Monthly Marketing Budget

Percentage of Annual Sales By Month	Projected Monthly Sales by Month	Projected Monthly Reserve 5% - 7%
Jan. _____%	$_____	$_____
Feb. _____%	$_____	$_____
Mar. _____%	$_____	$_____
April _____%	$_____	$_____
May _____%	$_____	$_____
June _____%	$_____	$_____
July _____%	$_____	$_____
Aug. _____%	$_____	$_____
Sept. _____%	$_____	$_____
Oct. _____%	$_____	$_____
Nov. _____%	$_____	$_____
Dec. _____%	$_____	$_____
Totals _____%	$_____ **Annual Budget**	$_____ **Annual Reserve**

Advertising Media Compared

The following should help you get an idea of the strengths and weaknesses of direct mail in comparison to some other media, by exploring the use of direct mail from "scratch" through a hope- fully successful result. This analysis will also be ideal for anyone considering using the mails to achieve a goal (selling, enlisting volunteers, promoting, etc.). For those who have tried direct mail before and been disappointed, you should make every effort to uncover the reasons why the mailing didn't work, so that future mailings will have better results. Even those who have been successful in direct mail may pick up some pointers moving forward. So, before any other consideration, is the decision to use direct mail instead of, or in conjunction with, other media.

Let's suppose that your media choices for an anticipated project are: TV, radio, billboard, newspaper, magazine, and direct mail, excluding telemarketing and broadcast faxes. There are a few other forms of media, which include: yellow pages, business directories, shoppers guides, and specialty advertising such as T-shirts. However, for this examination just consider the above for now. So, let's look at the strengths and weaknesses of each, which may be nothing new, but it is good to compare them side-by-side.

Television

TV is very generalized in its audience, and most advertisers must think in terms of their local TV stations rather than networks, and the best targeting locally is to schedule advertising during shows with certain appeals. Cost per thousand people exposed is very low. Production costs can be quite high. TV is powerful because of its nearly hypnotic qualities, but it has been more successful for reinforcement (i.e. soft drink ads do not try to get you to buy right now, they want you to think about their brand when you do buy) than for direct-response (call now 1-800-CALLNOW), but some direct response has proven to be successful on TV. Length of exposure is momentary and the number of exposures usually needs to be very high to get the saturation necessary for a return on investment. (How many times have you seen those *"try it...you'll like it"* commercials? Did they influence you?)

Radio

Radio allows you to target a more specific audience than TV, since most stations can be defined as Hard or Soft Rock, Top 40, Jazz, Oldies, etc., and stations can demographically identify their audiences somewhat, but still the audience is rather general. Radio has a low cost per thousand people reached, and also usually has low production costs. Radio is used mostly for reinforcement. Direct response is quite difficult because most people are driving, working, or playing when they listen to radio. Radio (or TV) can be used to support other media in your campaign, such as telling you to look for a coupon in your mail, newspaper, certain magazines, etc. As with TV, the length of exposure is momentary and the number of exposures usually needs to be high as mentioned above.

Billboards

Here again, this medium has a generalized audience. Areas of town can be targeted, and one strength of billboard advertising is in giving directions to your location. The cost per thousand people reached is low, but production cost can be expensive. Billboards are not very good for direct response. People can't remember phone numbers or addresses while they are driving. Billboard is good for supporting campaigns in other media. Length of exposure is momentary (unless people are stuck in traffic!). However, the general number of exposures are high.

Newspapers

Newspapers have a very generalized audience, although different sections of the newspaper can be used to target your audience. The cost per thousand people reached is low.

Production costs are usually low. Your ad is just one of hundreds hoping to gain attention. Newspaper can also be used for re-enforcing other media, announcements, or for direct response. Usually you do not have much room to get your message across. Coupons are a major strength in newspaper advertising. Length of exposure can be zero (most people do not read most ads) to several minutes if your headline or illustration can create enough interest for people to read further. Number of exposures are usually low except the classifieds, which is probably the most read section of the paper.

Magazines

This media gives you a good ability to target and verify your audience. Most magazines have a fairly well defined profile of their readership. However, although magazine lists provide good demographics, they cannot provide you with good psychographics (behavior data), meaning that just because a person reads *Better Homes and Gardens*, you cannot know their inclination to buy seeds through the mail. However, you can know that people on the customer list of Burpee Seeds are apt to buy seeds through the mail. Production costs are moderately inexpensive. Cost per thousand people reached is higher than for the previously mentioned media. Exposure time and space limitations are about the same as for newspapers with two exceptions: (1) that there are usually fewer ads competing with yours, and (2) while newspapers are normally only kept for a day or two, magazines are often kept indefinitely.

Direct Mail

Direct mail generally allows for more specialized and more widespread audiences than any other media. Direct mail can reach every home in any area with one exposure, which not even TV, radio, and newspaper can do with several exposures. Direct mail can be sent to super-precise lists, such as people who have bought gardening books through the mail in the last year in Rhode Island. Direct response is the strength of direct mail. Direct mail allows the presentation of more material than any other media. Direct mail allows for testing of different lists and different ads on a much smaller (i.e. cheaper) scale than any other media. The cost per thousand people reached in direct mail is relatively high, and so are production costs, considering printing and postage as production costs, but the response rate is much higher than other previously mentioned media. The number of exposures is usually a single individual, but direct mail often works better with several exposures.

Telemarketing

Unless you are calling an existing customer or responding to an inquiry, telemarketing is against the law in many states, and could incur you large fines. In many ways, this method of marketing is similar to direct mail in its characteristics. Business-to-business telemarketing and phone calls to a potential customer after an initial contact are usually acceptable, but "cold calling" people and soliciting especially calling them at home after a hard day at work - is considered rude at best and, as stated above, is illegal in most states. The cost per thousand exposures is high with telemarketing, and production costs are also high, due to the high time-consumption involved. Basically, business-to-business telemarketing works sometimes, business-to-consumer telemarketing will again, usually offend most people. So, be careful!

Summary

Most major organizations as well as small businesses are always interested in direct response. Unfortunately, many small-to-medium size businesses can't afford the luxury of simply trying to make people feel good about their company. We need measurable, fast results. In order to do that, we have to target our message to the people most likely to respond, make the response traceable, immediate, and repetitious. As you can see, that is very difficult with TV, radio, billboard, and even newspaper (except for actually being able to count the number of coupons returned). Those media are excellent for general announcements of sales, and for reinforcement. They can work for direct-response, but that is not their strength.

Media Planning Guide

The following is typical example of a monthly media planning guide that I suggest using to keep your budget on track as well as provide you with historical information for future planning.

Month of: _____

Activity or Media	Date	Description	Direct Cost	Production Cost
_____	_____	_____	$_____	$_____
_____	_____	_____	$_____	$_____
_____	_____	_____	$_____	$_____
_____	_____	_____	$_____	$_____
_____	_____	_____	$_____	$_____
_____	_____	_____	$_____	$_____

Sub Totals $_____ $_____

Total $_____

Prepared by: _____

Approved by: _____

Understanding PR & The Media

What Makes an Effective Press Release

The biggest challenge for most people who write PR is understanding what editors consider genuinely newsworthy and what they consider—blowing smoke. This misunder-standing is generally due to a lack of perspective of what the media considers newsworthy. Many marketing directors, product mangers, and CEOs, because they are so close to their organization's daily activities, think the whole world ought to care as much as they do about their company's every success. Save the self-serving laudatory for the weekly staff meeting. The press will see you as a pain in the butt if you issue non-news press releases too often, and they will eventually get to the point where they won't even bother to open an envelope with your company's return address.

What Isn't News?

All editors are guided by what is known in the media as the "BS Detector." With so many mediocre publicists trying to snow the press every day, this is a necessary defense mechanism. When you're evaluating whether or not to issue a press release, give it a thorough testing with your own BS-meter first. The following are some common topics that companies think the press should care about, and are then disappointed when they do not.

A New Web Site

This one is a matter of spin. Of course, the launch of a new online service should be a significant news event for most companies. The point is that the novelty of simply launching a Web site hasn't been newsworthy in and of itself since early 1995.

Upgraded Product

How compelling do you really find the words "new and improved" on a box of detergent or cereal? It's no more convincing as a news message than as an advertising pitch. Significant changes to your venture's business model might make interesting news.

Similarly, if you're a software company, do not count on mainstream media getting excited about your upgrade from a 2.0 product to version 3.0. Although, computer magazines and newsletters might take notice of this, but if your customers are in a non-technical industry segment, the publications that serve them are not likely to care about the new bells and whistles you have to offer. Acclaiming all the theoretical benefits doesn't cut it. The press wants installed users who can talk about good or bad observations, and not just about a few weeks of limited beta testing.

Staff Appointments

A new CEO is news, but may be a signal that there was something wrong with the old one. It might not be the best news to crow about without a well-considered spin. Unless they're major industry celebrities, your vice presidents, directors, financial officers, and the rest probably do not merit more than a brief in the local daily paper. Some publications do have "Movers and Shakers" or "People in the News" columns which you can target, but your A-list editors will probably value new-hire releases only as "ho-hum."

Gaining & Losing Customers

In our capitalist society, companies are in business to gain customers. Failing to so will subsequently force you out of business, and unfortunately, this is considered news. Getting new customers is business as usual, and not news. Unless the likes of an Intel or IBM, Ford or General Motors, or possibly the White House have standardized on your product, issuing a press release about bringing a little known customer on board is unlikely to spark interest from the press.

What Is News?

A good news story needs a hook. It should contain some sense of drama, importance, urgency, or righteousness. It may appeal to human interest, local pride, fascination with celebrities, or it could spark some interest due to humor, surprise, or irony slant.

Capitalize on Topical Issues

Stage an event, or introduce a feature focusing on something that's already prominent in the news or is destined to become so.

Issue an Industry Report

Find a topic related to your company's main theme, conduct a survey, and issue a report on the findings. Being the first to report about the percentage of women executives who are buying your product or service, for example, would certainly get you press exposure. Plus your findings are likely to be cited repeatedly over time. If this data is on your Web site many other sites may link to your survey from their pages. Continue to update the research monthly, quarterly, or annually, and your report could become a perpetual source of information and ultimately additional exposure for your company. Paying an outside consulting group to actually conduct the research would be money well spent, considering its genuine publicity value.

Hire a Celebrity Spokesperson

It is a very sad commentary about our society, but almost anything to do with a well-known personality seems to be newsworthy enough to almost guarantee you some press. If you can find some way of incorporating a big name into an association with your company, it is worth a press release.

Form a Strategic Partnership

Unlike winning a customer, partnering with another company can be newsworthy if the union brings a new level of value to your mutual customers and/or puts you in a stronger competitive position over industry rivals.

Bucking a Trend in the Industry

The press loves controversy! If everyone in your industry is jumping on the same band-wagon, be the first to charge loudly in the opposite direction. For example: the life of an Internet craze is normally a matter of weeks, so editors will tire of the latest overhyped fad quickly and be eager to give voice to someone who disagrees and why they disagree. Just be sure you can stand by your convictions, and do not set a corporate strategy based on a publicity opportunity that later turns out to be something that is not in the company's best interest.

Celebrate a Milestone or Contract Award

Do not overdo this idea, but large round numbers can be cause for attention. Celebrate your one-millionth customer, $10 million in revenue a year, or being awarded a contract with a large, well known corporation or government agency, in which many competitors were involved, and so on.

Present an Industry Award

Rise above being a mere player and become a judge of your industry's excellence.

Do Some Good Work for Society

Join a just cause, such as fighting a disease or raising money for a charity. Team up with organizations such as a mayor's office, a university, or, especially, other media outlets such as a newspaper or TV station, to champion a heart-warming cause. Your contribution could be no more than a promotion, but the event could provide you with substantial goodwill exposure.

Take a Political Stand

Is there a legislative debate affecting your industry? Boldly declare a position. Become a leading proponent of one side. Speak your piece at legislative hearings about the cause.

Found or Co-Found an Industry Association

Does your industry need to agree on common standards, or lack a body to represent its interests? Do not let someone else steal the thunder. Act first to get the ball rolling. If the association already exists, run for its top office. Show industry leadership!

Leveraging the Internet to Help Grow Your Business

Times Have Changed

Once there was life without drive-up fast food. Hard to imagine, but true. We called the local Burger King manager and asked, "How much of your business goes out the drive-up window?" "More than 50%," was the answer.

Opening a drive-up window must seem quite radical to restaurants that are used to a sit-down business. It involved a whole new way of understanding the food store business. But now it is taken for granted among the fast food giants. Doing business on the Web requires the same kind of quantum leap. It's hard to get your head around it right away, since it is so different from what you have been used to.

Opportunities for Your Business on the Internet

Newcomers see the Internet as advertising. But a business Web site is better understood as possibly a branch office or store, a place of doing business. It is like opening a second facility where you can entertain customers, except this facility has the lights on 24 hours a day, seven days per week. People can stop in at their convenience any time they want and browse through your offerings. They will:

1. Read promotional material.
2. Review "Common Questions People Ask About your Business."
3. Look at detailed information about the product or service you offer, and, if you have a vending machine in your lobby, make purchases day or night.

Additionally, no matter what business you are in, one thing is crystal-clear: you need to continue to expand sales and service to existing customers, find new customers, and make a profit in the process to keep your company growing.

Therefore, you need to constantly find new customers, because no matter how well you service your customers, you will lose some of them due to companies being merged or sold, turnover, closings, attrition, etc. This means you always have to develop new customers to replace the customer you lost in order to keep growing.

Your Web site should not only be a useful tool to provide existing customers and new prospects with information about who you are, what you do, and how well you do it, but should also be used to gather information from the new prospects who visit your site.

What's the monthly rent? Somewhere between $50 to $100 per month for smaller businesses. And the initial build-out of your branch office costs only a few thousand dollars. Sure, you'll need to remodel every month or two to keep it up-to-date, some sooner, others more often. But that is a small price to pay for the new customers your branch will bring.

Remember, do not think "advertising," think "branch office or store," and you will begin to grasp the Internet opportunity.

Direct Sales

Another opportunity is direct sales, jumping the existing distribution chain that ratchets up prices to the end user. Many online-only businesses are essentially order-taking front offices. Product fulfillment is through manufacturers and distributors who agree to drop-ship directly to the customer. This way the Web retailer does not incur expenses for inventory and warehousing. Direct retail sales via the Internet is growing exponentially. What an opportunity for your business!

Networking

Why does a company network its desktop computers? To increase communication, collaboration, and productivity. The Internet networks represent half the computers in the world!

Think of the possibilities. Small businesses can partner with others half a continent away to allow both of them to tackle contracts they could never handle alone. Virtual companies operate from inexpensive offices thousands of miles apart.
Talk about opportunities for your business!

Segmented Market

Better yet, this vast network automatically segments the market into demographic units. Want to market only to those searching for your particular product or service? Purchase a banner ad that pops up only when someone searches on "life insurance" for example, and you've suddenly begun to strike gold. What an opportunity!

Competitive Advantage

An Internet-savvy businessperson can be every bit as competitive on the Web as a 20, 200 or 2,000-employee business. It is harder than it used to be. Large companies now budget tens of millions of dollars for their Web sites. That's hard to match with a $2,000 to $20,000 small business Web site. But it's not impossible to do a very credible job, nevertheless. The market is so huge that even a small slice of this big pie can generate a quite substantial income for a small business. Opportunities are boundless.

Swiftness Equals Opportunity

These days it takes smarts and swiftness to compete with the Big Guys. The opportunity is surely here, but it is not a freebie.

Swiftness is the crucial ingredient. And here is where smaller businesses hold a big advantage. Changing from a strategy that is not working can take a big company months if not years. It's like turning an ocean liner. However, small businesses, like speedboats, can turn quickly and zoom off in a new and promising direction. The environment and business climate on the Web are changing so rapidly that you must be swift-footed to stay in business, and be ready to grasp the opportunities as they come. No points are awarded for being late.

The opportunities the Internet opens to your business are huge. If you apply smarts and swiftness you can transform these opportunities into your business success.

Advertising Your Business and Web Presence

How are companies using print advertising? You do not have to go far to see how some companies are trying to span the distance between print and the Internet. Many advertisers using print ads now include a URL.

Brochureware

Many businesses that sell off-the-shelf products can now sell directly over the Web. However, the sale of custom-built products and many services must be consummated with a telephone call. For high-ticket items, the final contract may be signed with a face-to-face meeting. For these businesses, a brochure format is an important part of the sales process. The purpose the brochure approach is severalfold:

1. To convey information needed to support the sale.
2. To help position the company in the mind of the reader.
3. To call for further action such as making a telephone call or sending an e-mail.

Level Playing Field

More and more large companies are moving to online sales on a daily basis. Nearly every savvy retail chain in the US is either on or will be on the Web as soon as it can. Is there room for the small businesses? Is the age of the level playing field over? Not yet!

Certainly the playing field has changed, and companies with some money to invest stand to gain. But smaller companies can certainly capture many of the specialty niches if they do so quickly.

Questions like: How can I get noticed? How can I get people to my site? Answer: aside from listing your site with the almost 400 search engines (Web Directories), the world purchases and reads periodicals in their areas of interest. Again, one much underutilized method is to use ads in print media to bring people to your online store or directly to your business location, That's where the eyes are. Capture them. And once in the door, its up to you to sell them your product or service.

Right now there is an excellent opportunity for fast-on-their feet business people to move into some of these niches and blind-side the old guard who do not understand how to use the Web to their advantage. With almost 80% of American homes on the Net, and many with a recent experience of online ordering they are ready, willing, and able to use the Web to do business with you either online or at your place of business.

General Internet Demographics: Are These Your Customers?

Gender

Females represent 38.7% of the respondents—users who have been online for less than a year (51.7% female, 48.3% male).

Educational Attainment

Although the average education level of web users has been declining to be more representative of the general population, respondents are still quite highly educated with 80.9% having at least some college experience and 50.1% having obtained at least one degree. Respondents who have been on the Internet for 4 years or more are much more likely to have advanced degrees (Masters & Ph.D.) than newer users.

Marital Status

The largest category of respondents are married (41.1%) and the next largest are single (38.7%).

Age

The average age for all respondents was 35.1 years. 36.4% of respondents are over 40 years old. The respondents with the most online experience tend to be in the 21-30 age range.

Major Geographic Location

As in all previous surveys, the majority of respondents are currently in the US (84.4%). The US also has the highest percentage of new users with 86.8% of respondents who have been online for less than a year.

Years on Internet

The largest category of respondents have been using the Internet in one form or another for 1 to 12 years (45%).

Respondents who have been online for less than a year represent 24.6% of females, but only 14.5% of males.

Household Income

The average income was $72,500 (US). 46.2% of respondents reported household incomes of $50,000 (US) or more. More experienced users tended to report higher income levels than new users (over $50K: 47.1% of experts, 30.7% of novices).

Primary Place of WWW Access

The majority of respondents access the Web exclusively or primarily from home (62.6%). Males are more likely to have access to the Web from several places (home and work) while females are somewhat more likely to access from just one place. The growth in home use of the Web is mainly fueled by people who used the Web at work & school and were transferring use into their homes, making it available to a new set of users (i.e. all the other members of their families).

Should You Out-Source Your Web Site Or Do It In-House?

With the availability of numerous software products from Microsoft, Adobe, and other easy-to-use Web page developing and editing software, a great many people are now trying their hand at it and many companies are seriously weighing whether or not they should prepare their company's Web pages in-house. Here are some of the issues:

Possible In-House Advantages:
1. Monetary savings
2. Knowledge increase stays with the company
3. Greater control over the final product
4. Ease in updating

Possible In-House Disadvantages:
1. Can't spare key people to learn HTML to level of excellence needed.
2. Do not have in-house graphics expertise or tools.
3. Can't spare key people to develop Internet marketing strategy without outside help.

Let's Look At Some of the Underlying Themes...

First, understand that the new software tools are deceptively simple. To make HTML accessible to the masses, programmers have decreased choices and limited access to the HTML code level. Sure, it's easier to do a good job, but nearly impossible to do an excellent job. The fallacy remains that these programs can't compensate for the user's inexperience.

Remember when desktop publishing programs were new? Suddenly you could produce print quality materials on your computer. But even though the tools were wonderful, but without graphic taste and experience, the final products were sometimes pretty dreadful.

However, a company's Web pages are not a computer thing, they are a communications thing. The stereotypical computer guru often doesn't have a sense of graphics or possess the marketing savvy necessary to make the project as successful as it could be.

Presenting your company's image on the Web needs a careful blend of graphic skill and taste, marketing savvy, and communication skills. Quite often, the individuals who might possess a combination of these skills are usually too busy with core business needs to spare the time, and for some companies the time investment in a team approach is sometimes prohibitive.

Rare is the company which has all the skills in-house. An outside Web page designer becomes part of that team, bringing skills and experience in disciplines vital to the overall success of the project.

Time:

First, you need to assemble and learn to use the essential software tools: an FTP program, a graphics program, and, get a grasp of some basic UNIX commands. You also need a user-friendly CGI script that transforms forms input into e-mail messages.

Do you really consider your time, or the time of your employees, to be valuable? From a time standpoint alone, outsourcing may really present a substantial savings initially.

Budget:

To do quality work you need quality tools. One of the most important tools...Adobe Photoshop, for example, sells off the shelf for about $600 or more. Without it your graphics will be lacking. Trust me; many companies have tried to work without it for way too long. Other costs are: increased memory to run a quality graphics program, a color scanner for photos and artwork, etc. Additionally, there is the question of hardware a good size Solaris system, say a SPARC 1000 with a robust storage array is often necessary to accommodate large quantities of information. The cost could range anywhere from $50,000 to $75,000 or more depending on your company's needs.

Effectiveness:

You also need to understand the Web well enough to develop an effective Web marketing strategy. That only comes with broad experience. The Web is already cluttered with thousands of sites that do not have more than an outside chance of being an effective tool in helping to grow their business.

The Web is a great leveler. Even a small business with only a few employees can compete on the Web head-to-head with the Fortune 500s of this world (but, only if they look as good and professional). In most cases, without professional assistance initially, you won't even come close to that kind of quality unless you are willing to invest a great deal of time, money, and human resources into the project.

The Alternatives:

There is a way to preclude the problem of paying for knowledge that doesn't stay with your company. You can contract a Web design firm to set up your initial Web site and provide maintenance for the first six months or longer, if necessary. Then assign one or more of your employees to learn to use the Web template and existing structure your designer has set up, to create other pages that look as good as the initial Web site. And, by all means, refuse to work with any designer who wants to retain copyrights, whose design will keep you dependent upon him or her for much longer than necessary.

Contract with someone who understands your goal to eventually bring Web page maintenance in-house. An experienced Web page design firm can:

1. Quickly produce a high quality Web site, good enough to hold its own against the best on the Net.

2. Work with you to bring on-going maintenance in-house during the first year.
3. Contract only with an experienced Web page designer who is also competent to advise you on Web marketing strategy.

When Should You Out-Source Your Business Web Pages?

1. When you do not have the specialized skills, equipment, and experience in-house.
2. When your quality standards are high.
3. When you really want to leverage your limited dollars and time.

When Should You Do It In-house?

1. Only **_YOU_** have the answer to that one!

How to Attract Visitors to Your Web Site

In today's market place you can't go on the assumption that "if-you-build-it-they-will-come." They won't! Once you build a Website you must give people a reason to come. A Website is a passive form of marketing, a guidepost so to speak, that points visitors to your products and/or services. To be effective, a Website should be considered a part of your marketing mix and promoted with several forms of marketing which we will examine below. So, let's cut to the chase...How do businesses with a limited budget attract visitors to their Web site?

List your Website with Web search engines that index the Web, such as Yahoo, Lycos, Web Crawler, Goggle and others. The actual registration process can be deceptively simple. A service called Submit It! (http://www.submit-it.com) provides a way to present information to approximately 15 of the most important search engines. I suggest that you do this late at night when Internet traffic is at its lowest. You can transmit your business's online address and description to all of these services in less than an hour. If you do this right, a person who is seeking your goods or services will quickly locate your name and Web address. Potential customers will have an opportunity to select your company from the increasing crowd of competitive vendors. The danger is that a carelessly-written 25-word marketing description can blow your opportunity to be seen by vast numbers of potential customers. This 25 word description must be written to include important key words so that customers will be able to locate your site. If you want to change your description from time to time, it can take as much as two to three hours to contact each of these services directly, and then beg, plead and yes, even nag them to make your changes.

There are several organizations that, for a small fee, will provide this service for you. You might want to start with these services on the Web at:

Promote It!
(http://www.camorg/~psarena/promote-it.html)
and WebPromote (http://www.stpt. com/shc /wp.html).

Give them a good reason to come. A well tested approach is to offer something of value for free. A number of well-financed corporate Web sites offer an entertaining fare which changes constantly. While most small business Web marketers can't afford to compete, you can afford to offer valuable information. If you take the time to provide up-to-date information about your industry, for example, you'll find people returning again and again to your site, each time increasing their chances of doing business with you.

A good approach to build traffic for your site is to barter industry-wide linking pages. You will want to consider negotiating a trade of links to and from other non-competing, but complementary sites. For example: If you sell camping equipment, you might contact sites that offer camping facilities. If you belong to a trade association they, more than likely will provide you with a list of their membership and would, more often than not, include a link to your site. If you put on your thinking cap you can, with a bit of effort, successfully develop a number of categories that would be worthwhile considering for an exchange of links or banners.

Be careful with whom you link and where you have links placed and where on your site you place links. You do not want to send visitors away from your site before they have an opportunity to see your wares and by the same token link to sites that make sense for your visitors to want to visit after leaving your site. Make sure that the links are functioning, the last thing you want to do is to frustrate your visitors by sending them off to never-never land. By the same token your links that reside on other sites should be checked for functionality and location. For example if you provide links on page three or four at your site, you should expect the same visibility or value in return.

Another choice is to purchase Web advertising on other high-traffic sites. A banner ad that will link to your site on a carefully-selected, high-volume Website is one way to get people to your site. A certain percentage of their thousands of visitors will explore your Website, and hopefully like what they find. A whole industry within the advertising agency industry has sprung up in the past few years that buys and sells advertising on the Web. Small businesses test the effectiveness of specific ads by the number of "click-throughs" from the site or sites where you have purchased space. Another way of checking, is to ask for an audit of actual page views where your banner resides. If you go the route of using an agency, I'm sure they will be able to answer many of your questions about buying or even selling advertising on your site. A word to the wise, talk to several companies before you make your choice. You will be surprised how differently they charge for their service and, if nothing else, you will get an education in the process.

You can let people know that your Website is to become active in several appropriate Internet news groups and mailing lists. Find the groups that are most likely to be frequented by your potential customers (groups can be narrowly or openly targeted, depending on the group). You might find groups that relate to your industry by doing a bit of research with SIFT, the Stanford Information Filtering Tool (http://hotpage. stanford.edu/), which searches messages about particular topics or companies voiced in thousands of news groups and mailing lists. "Lurk" for a few weeks so you understand the particular culture of the group you are targeting. Then find ways to add constructive comments to the discussion. At the bottom of each message include a "signature" (a 4-to 8-line mini-advertisement with your product, phone number, and Web address hot-link. Every time you contribute to the discussion, your mini-ad is seen by hundreds and puts them a click away from your site. You'll be surprised at the considerable response you might achieve this way, but like anything, it comes in proportion to hard work and persistence.

If it's appropriate, you may want to consider making your Website part of one or more of the many "malls." Businesses in physical shopping malls benefit from the traffic flow of the multitudes window-shopping. The same can be true online. Some malls only include businesses who subscribe to a particular Internet Service Provider (ISP) or pay a fee or percentage of their gross revenues. Others take any business that fits their particular criteria. Conditions and terms will vary from mall to mall. Here again, check out several for culture and traffic before making any decisions.

Be sure to include your e-mail and Web addresses on all your company's print literature, stationery, and display advertising. If people believe they can find out more about your products or services by looking online, many will do so.

There you have it! Any combination of the above should help to drive traffic to your site. Remember I said "combination" (its a synergy thing where 1+1=3 or 4, and so on). One will re-enforce the other, so use as many as possible for the best possible results.

Publicizing Your Web Site

Who cares??? In recent years publicizing the fact that your company has a new Web site has become a "ho-hum" issue. However, you should still send out press releases to all the media that reaches your audience, especially the publications where you might or do advertise. You just never know when you will spark some editors interest in using your press release. In some cases, I've known editors to use a "ho-hum" press release just to fill a blank hole on a page that needs to be filled. It would also not be unheard of to send your client base and prospects a copy of the release as well. After all this is the market you are trying to reach anyhow.

You certainly will want to notify your in-house staff and be sure to include human resources, product development, marketing, advertising, public relations, production departments, distributors or outlets for your product or service, the home office or parent company, and as I mentioned earlier at the top of the list be sure to notify the Web search engines such as Yahoo, Google, Net Search, and the hundreds of others that now exist.

All the departments and/or divisions within the company should also be encouraged to send you information that would be of interest to your customers, vendors, or prospective employees.

This baby you've created needs to be fed and nourished. Remember what was stated earlier, good Web sites are never static, they are dynamic and ever changing. New information about what your company or the industry or industries where you do business will keep visitors coming back and back again. So, use your imagination.

You might want to include and possibly subscribe to a few of the many magazines, newspapers or journals and that cover the Web.

Finally, be sure to include any membership or professional societies in your industry that produce a newsletter or journal.

Glossary of Web Terms

Anchor
A synonym for hyperlink

.aiff
A sound file format

.au
A sound file format

ASCII
(pronounced "Ask-ee") An acronym for American Standard Code for Information Exchange. ASCII essentially is plain, unadorned text without style or font specifications and it is easily transferred over networks.

Authoring Software
This is software that enables the creation of multimedia or hypertext documents and presentations.

Backgrounds
Think of the background as the type of paper you choose to print your brochure or advertisement on. This is simply a color you select that will appear behind your text and graphics on the computer monitor.

Bandwidth
This term describes the amount of data that can travel across telephone or network wiring. The larger the bandwidth the more information can be transferred over that network at one time. The term bandwidth also broadly includes throughput, meaning the amount of data sent. For reference look at the definitions for POTS, ISDN, T-1, and T-3.

Baud

The maximum speed at which data can be sent down a channel, or a unit of speed in data transmission. Baud is often equivalent to bits per second. Named after J. M. E. Baudot (died 1903).

BBS

This is an acronym for Bulletin Board System, a computer equipped with software and telecommunications links that allow it to act as an information host for remote computer systems.

Bit

A bit is the smallest unit of information that a computer can hold. It is a contraction of the words binary digit. Eight bits is equivalent to a byte. The speed at which bits are transmitted or bit rate is usually expressed as bits per second or bps.

Browser

A World Wide Web client that is more commonly known as a Web Browser. An information retrieval type of software that displays Web pages. The two most popular are: Netscape Navigator and Microsoft Internet Explorer.

Byte

The number of bits used to represent a character. Eight bits equal a byte.

CD-ROM

Compact Disc-Read Only Memory. It is used to store and play back computer data. A CD-ROM is an optical disk that can contain up to 650 MB of data. Use this term to refer to the actual discs but not the hardware you play the discs on. That is a CD-ROM drive.

Cern

The European Laboratory for Particle Physics. The originators of the HTTP and HTML concepts.

CGI
Common Gateway Interface. The CGI standard outlines the rules for running external programs in a Web server. External programs are called gateways because they open up an outside world of information to the server.

Client
The software that allows users the ability to retrieve information from the Internet and World Wide Web. NCSA Mosaic is an example of client software.

Cyberspace
This term was coined by William Gibson in his novel "Neuromancer." It refers to a near-future computer network where users mentally travel through tables of data. This has become a popular term which is now used to loosely describe the Internet, the World Wide Web, and many other computer networks. A much hipper term, but used the same way, is the "Information Superhighway."

Dial-up Connection
The most popular form of Net connection for the home user, this is a connection from your computer to a host computer over standard telephone lines.

Direct Connection
A permanent connection between your computer system and the Internet. This is sometimes referred to as a leased-line connection because the line is leased from the telephone company.

Domain Name
Domain names are issued by the Inter-NIC. They are assigned to individuals or companies seeking their own unique name on the Internet. They are used for electronic mail as well as Web site addresses. For instance if your name is Joe Smith, and your company name is Acme, your email address would be jsmith@acme.com and the Web site address or URL (Uniform Resource Locator) would be http://www.acme.com. Domain

names are issued with several different extensions to further identify what type of organization uses the domain. For example .com is for commercial establishments, .edu is for educational institutions, .gov is for a government body, .mil for the military and .org for nonprofit organizations. Some domains use geographical notations as well for example, .jp for Japan.

DNS
An acronym for Domain Name Server. DNS refers to a database of Internet names and addresses which translates the names to the official Internet Protocol (IP) numbers and vice versa. For example if you try to view a Web site at www.acme.com, the DNS will translate this URL into a series of numbers that is the official IP address which looks something like this: 202.237.113.27.

e-mail
This is an abbreviation for electronic mail. Email allows you to send and receive messages to and from other people around the world who also have email accounts. To have e-mail, you need to have 3 things. First your computer system needs to have a modem installed. Secondly you need to install software which allows you to send and receive messages. Thirdly, you need to set up an account with an email provider such as Netcom, AOL, AT&T or Microsoft ect..

FAQ
This is the acronym for Frequently Asked Questions. A common feature on the Internet, FAQs are files of answers to commonly asked questions. These files are designed to reduce calls and emails to support departments.

Firewall
This term refers to security measures designed to protect a networked system from unauthorized or unwelcome access.

FTP
File Transfer Protocol allows the transfer of files from one computer to another. FTP is also the verb used to describe the act of transferring files from one computer to another.

GIF
This acronym stands for Graphic Interchange Format, a commonly used file compression format developed by CompuServe for transferring graphics files to and from online services. A GIF file is limited to 256 colors.

Gopher
A text based distributed information system developed at the University of Minnesota.

GUI
An acronym for Graphical User Interface, this term refers to a software front-end meant to provide an attractive and easy to use interface between a computer user and an application. The Macintosh operating system has a GUI, DOS does not.

Home Page
The document displayed when you first open your Web browser. Home Page can also refer to the first document you come to in a Web site. The first page serves as the site's introduction, starting point, and guide. This starting point is often referred to as the Index page or Cover page.

History List
A list of Document Titles and URLs Mosaic keeps in memory that represents the visited URLs during a given online Internet session.

Hot lists
Lists of frequently used Web locations and URLs (Uniform Resource Locators).

Host
A computer acting as an information or communications server.

HTML

An acronym for HyperText Markup Language, HTML is the language used to format the documents on the World Wide Web. HTML uses formatting commands or "tags" that are embedded around the various parts of a Web document so browsing software will know how to display that document's links, text, graphics, and attached media. The tags do not appear on the browser screen, but translate the information for the browser.

HTTP

The abbreviation for Hypertext Transfer Protocol, HTTP is used to link and transfer hypertext documents.

Hyperlink

A link in a given document to information within another document. These links are usually represented by highlighted words or images. The user also has the option to underline these hyperlinks.

Hypermedia

Richly formatted documents containing a variety of information types, such as textual, image, movie, and audio. These information types are easily found through hyperlinks.

In-line Image

A graphic image that is displayed with an HTML document.

InterNIC

The abbreviation for Network Information Center, NIC is an organization, operated by Network Solutions, responsible for supplying information for component networks that comprise the Internet.

IP

The abbreviation for Internet Protocol, IP refers to the set of communication standards that control communications activity on the Internet. An IP address is the number assigned to any Internet-connected computer.

ISDN

The abbreviation for Integrated Services Digital Network. The ordinary telephone system doesn't handle large quantities of data, therefore the ISDN was established in 1984 to allow for wide-bandwidth digital transmission. ISDN is a telecommunications standard that uses digital transmission technology to support voice, video, and data communications applications over regular telephone lines. ISDN lines can transfer 64 kilobits of digital data per second.

ISP

Internet Service Provider, such as Netcom, Bell Atlantic, JUNO, AT&T, and others who provide connectivity to the Internet.

Java

Sun Microsystems' programming language for adding animation and other action to Web sites. The small applications (called applets) that Java creates can play back on any graphical system that's Web-ready, but your Web browser has to be Java capable for you to see it.

JPEG

The acronym for Joint Photographic Experts Group, JPEG is an image compression format used to transfer color photographs and images over computer networks. Along with GIF, it's one of the most common ways photos are moved over the Web. JPEG files can contain up to 16 million colors, therefore retaining a high degree of color fidelity.

Keyword

These words should appear on the first page of you Web site and allow search engines and browsers to easily locate your Web site. They also allow these search engines to easily categorize your Web site so that people looking for information on a particular subject will easily find your site.

Links

Links are the hypertext connections between Web pages. This is a synonym for hotlinks or hyperlinks, hotbuttons, or hypertextlinks. Links allow you to navigate throughout a Web site (internal links) or move about between different sites on the WWW (external links). Links are identified on a Web page because a word is highlighted in a different color, or a graphic/drawing/photograph has been programmed to link to another place. It is similar to turning the page in a book or moving from chapter to chapter in a book.

MIME

Multiple Internet Mail Extensions, a method of identifying e-mail files such as: that the first packet of information received by a client, contains information about the type of attached file the server has sent. For example: text, audio, movie, postscript, word document, etc....

Mosaic

This is the common name of a World Wide Web multimedia browser program developed at the National Center for Super-computing Applications in Urbana-Champaign, IL. The official, copyrighted name of the program is NCSA Mosaic™.

MPEG

The acronym for Moving Pictures Expert Group, MPEG is an international standard for video compression and desktop movie presentation. A special viewing application is needed to run MPEG files on your computer.

NCSA
The National Center for Supercomputing Applications. NCSA is located at the University of Illinois in Urbana-Champaign, Ill.

POP
An acronym for Point of Presence. POPs refer to the location where people can dial into an Internet provider's host computer that will allow you access the Internet. Most providers have several POPs to allow low-cost access via telephone lines.

Post Script
A page description language developed by Adobe Systems.

POTS
This is an acronym for Plain Old Telephone Service.

Protocol
A planned method of exchanging data over the Internet

QuickTime
A method of storing movie and audio files in a digital format. Developed by Apple Computer.

RFC
Request for Comments, they are the agreed upon standards with which all methods of communicating over the Internet are defined.

Search Engine
This term refers to a software program that helps users find information in databases. However, the term has more recently been applied to Internet companies such as: Yahoo, Snap, Excite, Lycos and others who will help you find Web sites and pages based on your quiry.

Server
A computer system that manages and delivers information for client computers.

SGML

Standard Generalized Markup Language, is an International standard, a encoding scheme for creating textual information. HTML is a subset of SGML

Shareware

This term refers to a concept of trying software prior to purchasing it. Shareware isn't software it is a way to distribute it. This software is available on public networks and BBSs. Users are asked to remit a small amount to the software developer, but it's on the honor system.

T-1

If an ISDN line doesn't handle enough data for you, this high-speed data line connection, a T-1 operates at 1.45 Mbps.

T-3

It handles almost 30 times more data than the T1 at 44.736 megabits of data transfer.

TCP/IP

Transmission Control Protocol/Internet Protocol, a set of rules that establish the method with which data is transmitted over the Internet between two computers.

TIFF

Tag Image File Format, a file format used in storing image files.

URL

This is the acronym for Uniform Resource Locator, the addressing system used on the World Wide Web. The URL contains information about the method of access, the server to be accessed, and the path of any file to be accessed. For example:http://www.acme.com is the URL for a company called Acme, Inc.

WAIS

Wide Area Information Server, a database

Webmaster
This term refers to the person in charge of administrating a company's World Wide Web site.

Web page
An HTML document that is accessible on the Web.

World Wide Web
Also known as The Web, WWW or W3, the World Wide Web is a hypertext-based Internet service used for browsing Internet resources.

XBM
X bit map, a simple image format. XBMs only appear in black and white and you will find them in-line in HTML documents.